The Legendary
DC-3

The Legendary
DC-3

Carroll V. Glines

and

Wendell F. Moseley

VNR VAN NOSTRAND REINHOLD COMPANY
New York   Cincinnati   Toronto   London   Melbourne

Library of Congress Catalog Card Number 78-31281
ISBN 0-442-26136-5 (cloth)
ISBN 0-442-26135-7 (paper)

Printed in the United States of America.

Published in 1979 by Van Nostrand Reinhold Company
A division of Litton Educational Publishing, Inc.
135 West 50th Street, New York, NY 10020, U.S.A.

Van Nostrand Reinhold Limited
1410 Birchmount Road
Scarborough, Ontario M1P 2E7, Canada

Van Nostrand Rinehold Australia Pty. Ltd.
17 Queen Street
Mitcham, Victoria 3132, Australia

Van Nostrand Reinhold Company Limited
Molly Millars Lane
Wokingham, Berkshire, England

16 15 14 13 12 11 10 9 8 7 6 5 4 3 2 1

Library of Congress Cataloging in Publication Data

Glines, Carroll V
  The legendary DC-3.
  Includes index. Edition for 1959 published under title: Grand Old Lady.
  Edition for 1966 published under title: The DC-3.
  Includes index.
  1. Douglas DC-3 (Transport plane) I. Moseley, Wendell F.,
  joint author. II. Title.
TL686.D65G55 1979   387.7'33'43   78-31281
ISBN 0-442-26135-7
ISBN 0-442-26136-5 pbk.

To Mary Ellen and Frances

who have waited and watched

for our Gooney Bird to come home

THE AUTHORS

Colonel CARROLL V. GLINES enlisted in the Army Air Forces as a flying cadet in May 1941. He was commissioned and received his wings on January 2, 1942 and during World War II served as a flying instructor and squadron and group commander.

In 1946 Colonel Glines was assigned to the Panama Canal Zone as an engineering officer and flew the C-47 regularly. At the start of the Berlin Airlift he was transferred to Germany. Upon his return to the States, he served as operations officer for a reserve training center, as assistant professor of air science (Air Force ROTC), as a faculty member at the Air Command and Staff College, Air University and at Headquarters, Air Materiel Command, Wright-Patterson AFB, Ohio. He was assigned to the Pentagon in January 1960 where he served in the Office of the Secretary of the Air Force and in the Office of the Assistant Secretary of Defense for Public Affairs. His final assignment before retirement in 1968 was as chief of public affairs for the Alaskan Command.

He is the author of 17 books, two of them with Lt. Colonel Moseley, and more than 500 magazine articles. He was formerly associate editor of *Armed Forces Management* magazine and editor of *Air Cargo*. He has been editor of *Air Line Pilot* magazine since 1971. He is a military command pilot, holds a commercial license and has flown more than 6,500 hours, many of those hours in the C-47/DC-3.

He holds bachelor's and master's degrees in management from the University of Oklahoma and a master's degree in journalism from the American University.

WENDELL F. MOSELEY graduated from the Army Air Forces Flying School in May 1941 and remained on active duty for over 26 years, retiring as a lieutenant colonel. During World War II he served forty-two months in the Pacific Theater of Operations as a pilot, flying many types of airplanes. Although he flew more than forty types of planes during his career, he remembers the old Gooney Bird (C-47) airplane as his favorite.

Other overseas tours included Panama and Saudi Arabia. In

Saudi Arabia he commanded an Air Rescue Flight and had rescue responsibility for eleven countries. At Patrick AFB in Florida he was a flying boat pilot for the Air Force Missile Test Center and flew several rescue missions while on this assignment. One open sea rescue with the flying boat saved the lives of three men who were stranded in a small boat in the open sea.

Other assignments included a tour as a member of the Air Command and Staff College faculty, and Chief of Information for the Fourth Air Force Reserve Region. He retired at Randolph AFB, Texas in 1967.

In addition to the books he has coauthored with Carroll V. Glines, Moseley has written for national magazines, has been a book reviewer, and once wrote short stories and a column for newspapers. He is also a professional landscape artist, and is presently Director of Development for The Air Force Village Foundation, Inc., San Antonio, Texas.

Other Books by Carroll V. Glines and Wendell F. Moseley

Grand Old Lady
Air Rescue!

Other Books by Carroll V. Glines

The Wright Brothers: Pioneers of Power Flight
The Saga of the Air Mail
From the Wright Brothers to the Astronauts
The First Book of the Moon
Doolittle's Tokyo Raiders
Four Came Home
Minutemen of the Air
Lighter-Than-Air Flight
The Compact History of the U.S. Air Force
The Modern U.S. Air Force
Polar Aviation
Helicopter Rescues
Our Family Affairs
The Complete Guide for the Serviceman's Wife
Jimmy Doolittle: Daredevil Aviator and Scientist

Foreword

FOR ALMOST HALF A CENTURY my time and energies have been devoted to the design and manufacture of commercial and military aircraft; and, for approximately the last half of that period, our organization has also undertaken research and production of missiles, culminating in our present work in the highly technical field of space equipment.

In 1921 the Douglas *Cloudster* took to the air. None of us who watched our initial model's first flight would have predicted the *Cloudster* would be followed by scores of designs and variations that have rolled from our assembly lines ever since. Each succeeding model was built for a specific type of flight duty, and I believe it reasonable to say in all due modesty that all of them were well-designed and successful aircraft.

A few of our designs attained some degree of fame, and one of them, the DC-3, has become almost legendary. It seems to go on forever. More than ten thousand of these transports were built, and several thousand remain in service today, representing a forty-year span of service. It is fairly safe to predict that a few of these hardy veterans will be flying at the half-century mark.

There is a warm and permanent place in my affections and memories for this airplane, and an even warmer sense of respect for the airline operators, the technicians, and all the commercial and military pilots who have worked and lived with these ships in all corners of the world. To these men must go the largest measure of credit for the multiple exploits, the almost incredible adventures, and, even more important, the solid years of dependable and workaday accomplishment that combine to perpetuate the DC-3 legend.

DONALD W. DOUGLAS, SR.

ACKNOWLEDGMENTS

IN SEARCHING OUT THE MATERIAL for this history of the most famous airplane in the world, we found that there are hundreds of people who have tales to tell about the Grand Old Lady of the Skies. Our task eventually became one of choosing the best of the stories rather than trying to locate them. We wrote hundreds of letters and pored over a thousand photographs. Everywhere we turned there was something that should be mentioned in a book about the DC-3. Sadly, only a small fraction of these stories and photographs could be retained here.

The person who helped most in locating the material was Joe B. Messick, public relations representative for Douglas Aircraft Co. His Photo Librarian, Mrs. Ida Herschensohn, patiently spent many hours with us while we researched her well-kept selection of photos. Harry Gann, current historian for Douglas, was particularly helpful in preparing Appendix 1. Others also helped and we are grateful to them: Donald W. Douglas, Sr.; Donald W. Douglas, Jr.; General Maxwell D. Taylor; General Anthony C. McAuliffe; Colonels Frank J. McNees and Troy Crawford; Lieutenant Colonels Charles A. Rawls, Perry C. Emmons, Donald A. Shaw, and Paul C. Fritz; Majors Robert C. Mikesh, Annis G. Thompson, Archie G. Burdette, Harold T. Allen, Frank Sweeney, Donald V. Browne, and Francis L. Satterlee; and Master Sergeant Walter E. Jones. Publicists of the major airlines also contributed stories and photos.

Because we did not include all the stories and photos received from all over the world in this book, it does not mean that we are ungrateful. When one considers the vast areas over which the airplane has flown, and the millions of people who have either flown it or flown in it, it is understandable that many volumes could be written about the feats and accomplishments of this wonderful machine. To all those who so kindly sent us material, we gratefully tender our thanks for their interest in the finest airplane that ever was or ever will be built by man.

C.V.G.
W.F.M.

Contents

Introduction

DURING THE LAST SEVEN AND ONE-HALF DECADES the world has seen literally thousands of different kinds of airplanes come and go. In this time, four big wars and scores of small ones have proven the airplane to be a valuable weapon. Between wars, the airplane has become an instrument of peace. It is now universally recognized that no more wars will be fought and no peace truly lasting without the airplane playing a dominant role as an instrument of power—either military or economic. In just the short span of a man's lifetime, the airplane has changed from a symbol of folly and daring to a symbol of strength and national vigor.

Of all the airplanes ever built that have contributed in some measure to aviation progress, there is one which has far surpassed all others in faithful service, dependability, and achievement. It has been parked on the ramps of the world's air terminals for over forty years. It was born during the days of wooden propellers and is still flying as we pass from the jet age into an era of space flight.

This book is about that airplane: its birth, its development, its adoption by the airlines and the military services, its uses in World War II, Korea and Vietnam, its conversion to civilian use after the wars, its innumerable feats as an angel of mercy, its employment as a jack-of-all-trades, and, finally, its future.

This fabulous airplane has earned many names, set many records and scored innumerable aviation "firsts." It has flown more miles, piled up more flying time, carried more cargo and passengers, and performed more "impossible" feats than any other winged craft in the world. The manufacturer called it the *Skytrain* and designated it the "DC-3." The airlines call it simply, "the Three." The U.S. Air Force called it the "C-47." The U.S. Navy called it the "R4D." The Birtish called it the *Dakota*. But these are official names. The men who fly this extraordinary machine have other names for it. Airline pilots call it the "Dizzy Three." Civilian pilots and passengers have given it such names as "Old Methuselah," "Placid Plodder," and "Dowager Duchess." Today, however, pilots everywhere refer to it with great affection as the "Gooney Bird" after the albatross, whose great powers of flight and ubiquity are legendary.

We fell in love with the Gooney Bird when we were still teen-agers, while watching it come and go at our local airports. We dreamed of the day when we might fly one of these magnificent, stately birds. The great day came for both of us when we won our wings as pilots in the U.S. Army Air Forces. We early formed an attachment for this ingenious collection of aluminum, rivets, wires and gadgets as much as anyone can become attached to an inanimate object.

This plane, of all the planes we have flown, doesn't seem inanimate, somehow. It has a distinct personality, a warmth, an identity, and even a nobility that is unlike anything else man-made we know of. It is dependable, forgiving, attentive, gracious and benevolent. The plane was here when we both entered the service nearly four decades ago. It is still here as good as new now that we have ended our military careers. We have flown it for thousands of hours. We have had our moments of doubt, but we have always come home—safely and full of gratitude for the qualities that have been built into the Grand Old Lady of the Skies.

We hope we can convey to the reader in the pages that follow what a remarkable flying machine Mr. Douglas built. If so, we will have partially repaid the kindly Gooney Bird for the years of progress it has brought to the flying art and the many hours of pleasure we have had when it was in our hands. But let no man think this book is a eulogy for the deceased. The Gooney Bird is still in the prime of life, and will outlive us all.

"There isn't a plane in the world..."

1

. . . all of us on the airlines had a great respect for the Three. It, as no other aircraft, aided us in preparation for the ships of today and those to come.

—CHARLES W. MEYERS
Captain, Eastern Air Lines

CAPTAIN WARREN C. TOMSETT, thirty-three-year-old pilot of the C-47 code-named *Extol Pink* stalked briskly out into the damp, pungent air of the Vietnamese night. Behind him in single file followed his copilot, Captain John Ordemann, navigator Captain Donald Mack, Technical Sergeant Edsol Inlow, and loadmasters Jack Morgan and Frank Barrett. They had just been briefed to fly a flare drop mission in support of operations by South Vietnam ground forces against the Viet Cong Communist guerrillas.

After three years of unofficial war, the United States Air

Force had perfected a system of co-ordination with the Vietnamese to counter the night terror raids on their fortified hamlets. It had been a truism among the villagers that they felt reasonably safe during the day but "the night belongs to the Viet Cong!"

Communist guerrilla strategy had been simple: intimidate and terrorize the helpless South Vietnamese into submission and spread communism further into Southeast Asia. Surprise night attacks had been the most successful tactics used. The hard-pressed South Vietnamese Government pleaded for some method of nullifying or preventing the nightly raids. The United States Air Force, committed to a national policy of advising the anti-Communist governments in air matters, came up with an answer to this vexing problem: USAF pilots could not fire on the Viet Cong enemy unless fired upon first. They could, however, fly non-offensive reconnaissance missions. The result was an operation nicknamed "Night Angel" which proved to be the salvation of many outposts and strategic hamlets. Aircraft equipped with "paraflares" could maintain an all-night vigil in the skies overhead. When a call for help was received from a besieged outpost, the plane would envelop the scene below in an umbrella of light. Often all that was needed to halt the attack was the brilliant illumination provided by the flares. If the attack continued, Vietnamese Air Force fighters from nearby bases were scrambled to make strafing and bombing attacks on the Viet Cong positions. From the time of the first flare drop mission, the night no longer belonged to the Viet Cong.

The aircraft chosen for the flare drop missions was not a new plane especially designed for this kind of mission. It was an ancient craft, more than a hundred years old when reckoned by the expected life span of the average airplane. It was a 150-mile-an-hour transport plane with the simple military designation of "C-47" which had been designed in the 1930s and had seen war service all over the world since. It proved to be the only airplane for the job in war-torn Vietnam.

The C-47 assigned to Captain Warren Tomsett that night of

July 20, 1963, was an old faithful C-47 with over 10,000 hours on its airframe that had been built in 1945 and earmarked for the scrap pile a decade later. It had never got there because a newer replacement type of aircraft could not be found. The C-47 has been dubbed "the airplane that won't wear out" and there are over three decades, billions of passenger miles, and thousands of pilots to vouch for that. Warren Tomsett didn't know it but he was on a mission that would win the Distinguished Flying Cross for himself and his copilot, and Air Medals for the rest of his crew. More than that, it would win for them the Mackay Trophy as "The Most Meritorious Flight of the Year."

Captain Tomsett lifted his lumbering Gooney Bird into the black sky above Bien Hoa a half hour before midnight and headed southwest over the lush delta area to his assigned patrol sector. He was in constant touch with the Air Operations Center at Bien Hoa as he cruised through the darkness guided only by the ground controller's instructions. The navigator sat at his table behind the pilots, keeping track of the plane's position, while the loadmasters in the rear listened on the interphone for instructions to throw out the flares. It looked like the beginning of a long night.

"Extol Pink, this is Paris Control," a voice on the radio announced with a practiced calmness born of long experience. "Will you accept a rescue mission, repeat, rescue mission? Over."

Tomsett stiffened in his seat and grabbed the mike. "Roger, Control, understand you want me for rescue mission. What's the urgency? Over."

"Six critically wounded personnel need immediate evacuation' from Loc Ninh. Will you accept the mission? Over."

Tomsett had never heard of the airstrip at Loc Ninh. He was told it was only 3,600 feet long and 65 feet wide. Located 75 miles northwest of Saigon, it was only 8 miles from the Cambodian border. It had been hacked out of the virgin jungle with trees 200 feet high forming an impenetrable wall at both ends of the runway. Daylight landings at Loc Ninh were bad enough, but night operations were deemed impossible because of the mountainous terrain and the lack of landing lights and navigational aids. Just to locate it in the pitch blackness would take extraordinary navigational skill. To make a landing and a take-off would require all the skill—and guts—ever mastered by a pilot in wartime. Six Vietnamese lay dying near that strip. They would never see daylight if Tomsett refused to try. And no one would ever blame him if he refused to risk his life and the lives of his five crewmen to save the lives of an equal number of men he didn't know and whose language he could not speak.

"We'll take it," Tomsett said firmly. "Are you sending up a relief flare ship? Over."

"Roger. Remain in your area until relieved in about one hour."

Tomsett turned the controls over to Ordemann and left his seat to talk to the navigator, Captain Don Mack. A former weatherman, the thirty-six-year-old Mack had completed navigation school in 1958 and had joined the 1st Air Commando Wing in 1961. "Look up Loc Ninh, and tell me everything you can about it," Tomsett told him. "Then give me a course and an estimated time of arrival [ETA] over the strip."

While Mack worked, Tomsett instructed Sergeant Inlow, the flight engineer, to verify the fuel consumption on both engines and discussed with the loadmasters, Sergeants Morgan and Barrett, what they were to do to help load the wounded aboard.

By the time Tomsett had briefed Morgan and Barrett, Don Mack had finished his research. He gave his pilot a thorough briefing on headings, terrain features, location of other airstrips and known Viet Cong concentrations, the magnetic heading to follow, and the ETA over Loc Ninh.

At 2:30 A.M. *Extol Pink* was relieved by a Vietnamese flare ship and headed on the course Mack had plotted. When scattered clouds started to form at 500 feet above the ground, Tomsett knew he had to get below them. The visibility decreased as the clouds thickened. There were no lights or visible landmarks outside. Radar contact with the Operations center was lost as the plane's low altitude took it off the radar-scopes. Tomsett could only fly the course Mack had prescribed and wait until the ETA was up.

"Two minutes to go for ETA," Mack suddenly announced.

The other five crew members stared through the blackness, looking for some sign of an airfield ahead.

"You should see it dead ahead. . . . Now!" Mack said as he watched the second hand on his watch creep around the dial.

Sergeant Inlow, standing between the pilot and copilot, was the first to see several small fires outlining a runway directly under the nose of the aircraft. "There it is!" he shouted, pointing below.

Tomsett wheeled the C-47 into a left turn and studied the ill-defined runway he was expected to land on. The field was so small and poorly marked and the weather had deteriorated so badly that had Mack's navigation been off by even an eighth of a mile the crew would never have seen it. Its proximity to the Cambodian border had presented further demands on his skill since overflight would have caused an international incident.

Tomsett planned his approach carefully. He used full flaps and a steep, near-stall glide to insure missing the trees at one end of the runway and stopping before he reached the other end. On the approach he could see tiny flashes of light winking through the jungle foliage. The Viet Cong had completely surrounded the strip and were peppering away at the plane with small arms fire.

The official report of the mission stated simply that the "landing was accomplished under blackout conditions," which meant that Tomsett's only reference to the ground was the light made by the tiny fires (actually two rolls of toilet paper jammed on sticks and soaked in gasoline) placed erratically on both sides of the strip. He taxied to the end of the strip and shut down the engines while the wounded were loaded aboard. An attempt was made to inspect the plane for battle damage, but since no lights could be used and another Viet Cong attack might come at any moment, Tomsett decided that as long as his controls and engines responded, he would try the take-off.

Captain Don Mack and the three sergeants immediately started improvising litters as there was only one aboard the aircraft. These were hastily made from parachutes and bamboo poles, and the six wounded Vietnamese were carried aboard, all in critical condition.

The loading door was slammed shut as Tomsett started the engines and did a 180-degree turn on the runway. He decided to take off in this opposite direction to avoid staying too long on the ground. As he checked the engines, he discovered that the center instrument panel lights had failed and he couldn't see the instruments. Sergeant Inlow, an old hand at improvising, whipped out his flashlight and held its beam on the panel. "Let 'er go, Captain!" Inlow shouted.

Tomsett jammed both throttles forward to the stops, held the brakes momentarily and headed the lumbering transport down the narrow strip. Once again, automatic weapons fire was seen winking out of the darkness, but the blacked-out ghostlike plane was hard to see. Putting the creaking Gooney Bird into a maximum performance climb, the daring pilot escaped both the bullets and the murderous trees at the end of the runway.

En route to Saigon a U. S. Army medic, who had decided to come along at the last minute because of the precarious condition of the Vietnamese, Captain Mack, and the three sergeants cared for the wounded. By the time the plane arrived at Saigon, their uniforms were covered with blood. Colonel Gerald J. Dix, commander of the 1st Air Commando Wing, reported:

After the wounded were delivered to the waiting ambulance the crew of *Extol Pink* returned to Bien Hoa at 0455, almost seven hours after their original scramble. Each member of the crew had contributed unselfishly to the success of both missions. Their professional performance, adaptability, and courage reflect great credit upon their country and the United States Air Force. Their efforts and gallantry helped to save the lives of comrades in arms in the fight against the common enemy and added immeasurably to the morale and effectiveness of the Army of South Vietnam.

I consider this the most meritorious flight of the year. The entire crew exposed themselves to hostile action throughout the flight. The professional skill, daring and extraordinary heroism displayed by the entire crew was instrumental in the success of the mission.

General Curtis E. LeMay, Air Force Chief of Staff, agreed with Colonel Dix's observation and presented the modest sextet with the Mackay Trophy. Neither Warren Tomsett nor any of his crew members believe they should get all the credit for the success of their mission. "It's the airplane that earned the trophy," they say. "We just made it do what it has been capable of doing for many years. There isn't a plane in the world that could match it!"

The feat performed by the crew of *Extol Pink* in their C-47 was just one more in the unending saga of "impossible" accomplishments by an airplane that refuses to grow old. The C-47 that clawed its way into the safety of the skies that night in Vietnam was, according to the experts, long overdue for the scrap heap. It had been flying for twenty years (twice the lifetime of most military planes) for the Air Force, as each year it and its hundreds of sister ships were given a reprieve so that they could keep on doing their jobs which, apparently, no other plane can do. Each year a replacement has been sought for the aging Methuselah of the skies. Each year the world's plane manufacturers sheepishly admit that none can be found. The airplane—the magnificent DC-3 and its military versions, the C-47 and R4D—has become a legend in its own time.

From whence did this legend spring? What is the origin of this airplane that refuses to die? What manner of genius could design a plane that could haul 600 million passengers and millions of tons of cargo for ten billion miles and still show no signs of wearing out? It all began with the DC-1.

The single most important date in the history of the Douglas Aircraft Company is August 2, 1932. It was on this date that Jack Frye, vice president in charge of Operations for Transcontinental and Western Air, a vigorous but desperate young airline, wrote letters to several aircraft manufacturers. It was a two-paragraph letter soliciting bids for "ten or more trimotor transport planes." TWA's specifications were clearly stated: an all-metal monoplane with a maximum gross weight of 14,200 pounds, a fuel capacity for a cruising range of 1,080 miles at 145 miles per hour, with the capacity to haul 12 passengers plus a crew of two. Frye's letter ended with the simple question, "Approximately how long would it take to turn out the first plane for service tests?"

One of Frye's letters was addressed to Donald W. Douglas, thirty-eight-year-old president of the Douglas Aircraft Company, Santa Monica, California. Others were sent to Curtiss-Wright, Ford, Martin, and Consolidated. The reason for Frye's invitation to the aircraft industry was obvious to all the recipients. The great Knute Rockne, famed Notre Dame football coach, had been killed on a TWA Fokker F-10 en route from Kansas City to Wichita, Kansas, on March 31, 1931.

Public condemnation of air travel was prompt and deserved, with the brunt of the reaction aimed at TWA and its ancient plywood and fabric-covered Fokkers. TWA turned to the all-metal Ford trimotors, which were but little improvement and certainly were not comfortable or economical to operate. TWA was desperate and now turned to the budding industry as a whole to help it survive.

Donald Douglas has called the letter from Frye "the birth certificate of the DC ships" and deservedly so. As soon as he digested its contents he called in his staff of engineers and production men: J. H. ("Dutch") Kindleberger, Arthur E. Raymond, Fred Herman, Lee Atwood, Ed Burton, Fred Stineman, and Harry E. Wetzel. Together they pored over the specifications and came to some astounding conclusions. New, more powerful engines under development, new techniques in metal construction that were coming along, and innovations in metal propellers might be combined to make an entirely new airplane. In ten days of around-the-clock figuring, Douglas and his experts concluded that they could not only meet Frye's specifications but could exceed them. The

plane they envisioned would be designed for passenger comfort
as well as speed and safety. A retractable landing gear would
be designed which would fold into the engine nacelles for
better streamlining. But unique among its innovations was that
it would be a low-wing monoplane with semi-monocoque
fuselage and would be powered by only two engines instead
of three. This time, though, they were going beyond the state
of the art by proposing a "honeycomb" wing construction and
the partial stressing of wings and fuselage with aluminum skin.

Designing planes that were different was not strange to this
unusual collection of engineering talent. The same men had
teamed up with Douglas in the early Twenties and had
engineered and built a whole stable of Douglas planes. First
was the *Cloudster*, designed, built and flown in 1920. Four
years later came the *World Cruisers* in which U. S. Army Air
Service flyers made the first aerial circumnavigation of the globe.
Then followed the C-1 and then the M-1, -2, -3, and -4—the
first planes specifically designed to carry mail.

It was decided that Harry Wetzel, general manager, and
Arthur Raymond, then the assistant chief engineer, would take
the train to New York. Still with much work to do, they bundled
their sketches and notebooks full of figures under their arms
and boarded the Pullman. As the countryside sped by, the two
engineers kept working. Two weeks after Douglas had received
Frye's letter, Wetzel and Raymond presented the Douglas
design proposal to a TWA group, which included Frye, Richard
W. Robbins, TWA president, and its most famous stockholder
and chief technical adviser, Colonel Charles A. Lindbergh.

The TWA group was fascinated by the Douglas sketches.
This was not only a new plane but a new concept of aircraft
design as well. "I like it," Frye said. "What do you think, Slim?"

Lindbergh was thoughtful for a moment. He remembered
the tragedy of the Fokker that killed Knute Rockne. "I
recommend that we accept the concept, but Douglas must
make one guarantee in addition to meeting the specifications.
This ship should be able to take off with a full load from any
point on the TWA route *on one engine!*"

Wetzel and Raymond looked at each other and took out their slide rules. The answer, as Raymond recalls it today, was only about 90 per cent Yes. The remaining 10 per cent could only be assured by actual test. "We'll try," was all Raymond could say.

The contract between Douglas and TWA was signed on September 20, 1932, and new life surged through the Douglas shops. The plant had been shut down, with only a skeleton force kept around to keep the rust off the machinery. The Depression had hit the budding aircraft industry hard. There was real cause for rejoicing when it was announced that Douglas was hiring its old hands back.

Weeks followed without any visible sign of an airplane being born. Then, slowly, the various shops began to get the blueprints from which they were to make the thousands of parts that go to make up an airplane. Each print was marked mysteriously with the code "DC-1" which meant "Douglas Commercial—1st Model."

The fuselage, bigger and longer than a Greyhound bus, gradually began to take shape on the assembly floor. As each skin panel was carefully fitted into place, the excitement among the employees rose. It was a graceful thing, but it seemed so big. When the vertical stabilizer and wings were fitted on, it *was* a big airplane—the largest twin-engined landplane built in this country up to that time.

The shiny aluminum sparkled in the sunlight as the huge craft was pushed out of its hangar on June 22, 1933. Sleek and smooth in shape, it looked like a giant eagle as it was guided to the center of the parking ramp. The fuselage measured 60 feet from nose to tail and the wings stretched 85 feet from tip to tip. The nose tilted toward the sky as the plane rolled on its two main wheels and smaller tail wheel. Two Wright Cyclone 710-horsepower, nine-cylinder, air-cooled radial engines were fitted to the forward edges of the wings. Three-bladed Hamilton propellers, whose pitch could be controlled in the cabin by the pilot, were attached.

Inside the cabin were two rows of six seats in tandem with

a broad aisle between. A small galley was located near the door for preparing meals in flight. In the rear was a lavatory and toilet, another "first" in passenger comfort. Passengers could stand up and walk around in the cabin. Soundproofing insulation had been installed and cabin heaters to overcome the well-justified complaints of those who had ridden the Fords, Fokkers, and Boeings.

In the cockpit were more innovations. Dual controls and side-by-side seating for the pilots had been provided. New gyroscopic instruments were installed that would make blind flying easier and safer. Included was the new Sperry automatic pilot which could enable the pilot to fly "hands off"—the first commercial plane to be so equipped.

But beautiful and big as it was, one question remained uppermost in everyone's mind: Would it fly?

The day was bright and clear, and a slight breeze was blowing off the ocean. The calendar on the wall of the flight-line maintenance shed read Saturday, July 1, 1933. A group of mechanics busied themselves around the shed. To them the first flight of a new airplane meant hours and sometimes days of tinkering with engines, fuel lines, pumps, and the hundreds of little things that, if neglected, can mean the difference between life and death. No mechanic ever born wants to be responsible for doing or not doing something that could cause death or injury to a crew.

It had been announced that the first flight of the DC-1 would be made by Carl A. Cover, test pilot and vice president in charge of Sales. Cover, attired tastefully in a tweed suit and a bright green hat, climbed aboard with Fred Herman, a project engineer who was on the DC-1 as copilot. Crowds of people were lined up on both sides of Santa Monica's Clover Field runway. Santa Monica residents had gotten used to Douglas "first flights," but somehow there was always the same fascination. Everyone wanted to see if this new Douglas bird would fly—and if so, how well.

Cover busied himself in the cockpit, checking switches,

hydraulic pressure, and instrument readings. When both men were secure in their seats, Cover leaned out his window and shouted "Clear!"

A mechanic standing on the left side, hand on a fire extinguisher, gave him the signal indicating that all was clear. Cover touched the starter switch on the port engine. The starter snarled. The propeller turned a few revolutions. Then the engine fired and broke into a roar. The other engine was started and Cover taxied into take-off position.

After running the engines up, checking controls, and making a last-minute check of his safety belt, Cover pulled out onto the runway. Instead of taking off, however, he taxied up and down the runway, testing brakes and, again, controls and engines. Finally he nosed the giant plane into the wind, opened the throttles wide and headed down the field.

The gleaming craft, full of life, sped straight ahead, a beautiful sight in the early morning sun. The tail came up, slowly, then the main wheels came off the ground at exactly 12:36 P.M. The engines purred as smoothly as a new watch.

Suddenly, without warning, just as Cover pulled into a climb, the left engine sputtered and quit. The crowd gasped. A woman screamed. The craft nosed down momentarily and, as it did, the engine caught again. The crowd sighed. Cover cautiously lifted the nose and, as he did, both engines quit with that awful silence, the full meaning of which all pilots can appreciate. Again Cover jammed the nose forward, and again the twin engines roared back to life.

Cover, his hands busy in the cockpit, had no time to think. He was an old hand at the flying game and his reflexes saved his life. The reflex that told him to get the nose down when he lost an engine was the very reflex that made the engine cut back in again. The second time it happened he reasoned that he would have to climb carefully. He nursed the craft slowly to 1,000 feet and started his turn. The engines were sputtering and he decided to land the plane in a nearby field rather than risk a complete traffic pattern.

As the airplane disappeared behind the hangar, the crowds gasped, sure that they would see a billow of smoke and hear the heart-rending sound of metal crashing to earth. But no noise was heard and no smoke appeared. The people turned to one another and, with questioning looks, started to speculate on what had happened. Douglas engineers rushed to their cars and disappeared in the direction where they had last seen their "baby."

Cover had made a successful, controlled landing with no damage to the airplane. As he and Herman climbed out, a little pale and visibly shaken, the first car, containing engineers, roared up.

"What happened, Carl?" they asked in unison.

"The dad-blamed engines cut out. That's all I know. Every time I tried to get the nose up, she cut out. I think you'd better check those carburetors. There's something screwy in Denmark." Cover wiped the perspiration from his forehead.

Engineers swarmed over the engines after the airplane was towed back to Clover Field. It was some time before they discovered that the experimental carburetors were to blame, just as Cover had suggested. The floats were hinged in the rear, thus shutting off the gas whenever the nose of the craft was pulled up into climbing position. The carburetors were turned 180 degrees, and the trouble was permanently corrected.

For the next six weeks, the DC-1 was subjected to the most intensive series of tests any Douglas plane had ever had to endure. Company test pilots, TWA pilots, and Jack Frye himself, a fully qualified airline pilot, wrung it out so much they were amazed that no structural failures showed up.

But the test program for X223Y—the number given to the plane by the U. S. Department of Commerce—was not without incident. On one occasion a mechanic put heavy engine oil in the automatic pilot instead of hydraulic fluid and the controls became so stiff that it took the full strength of both pilots to get the plane back on the ground. On another occasion, with test pilot Eddie Allen at the controls, the landing gear was forgotten in a mix-up of cockpit signals and a belly landing was made. The only damage, however, was a pair of bent props and the egos of two red-faced pilots.

Test after test was conducted and the DC-1 passed them all.

Then the day came for the plane to pass the test Lindbergh had added—the single-engine take-off. It was September 4, 1933. Eddie Allen was the pilot, and D. W. Tomlinson was copilot. They had selected Winslow, Arizona, as the test site, since its elevation was 4,500 feet above sea level—the highest airport on the TWA route. Air is thinner at higher altitudes and engines have to work harder to get the plane in the air. The higher the altitude, the less efficient an engine becomes— the less power it will produce—and thus the tougher the test would be. Allen gave full throttle to both engines and the loaded plane slowly gathered speed. Just as the wheels left the ground, Tomlinson reached up and cut the ignition switch on the right engine. The plane lurched to the right, but Allen caught it in time and the ship held course straight ahead. Slowly but surely the half-powered plane climbed to 8,000 feet and leveled off. Still flying on one engine, Allen flew to the next stop on the route, Albuquerque, New Mexico—240 miles away. Not only did the One make it in good time but it arrived 15 minutes ahead of a Ford trimotor which had departed from Winslow before the DC-1. If there were any doubts about the DC-1 before this test, they were now completely swept away. TWA accepted the one and only DC-1 ever built and immediately placed orders for twenty-five more with slight structural changes. The wings were to have ten feet more spread to support a longer fuselage which was to carry fourteen passengers instead of twelve.

When the order arrived and the new specifications studied, Douglas engineers realized they were designing a new airplane and designated it the DC-2. The DC-1 contract price was $125,000, but it had cost Douglas $300,000 to build. The original agreement was that TWA would have an option to buy up to a total of sixty planes at $58,000 each. The net result was that Douglas lost over a quarter of a million dollars on the first order of twenty planes. Being a farsighted individual, however, and with the promise of future aircraft deliveries to other airlines, Douglas gambled that he would one day recoup his losses.

Although TWA started getting delivery of the DC-2's within a few months, the line continued to use the DC-1 for experimental purposes. It became known to the press as the "laboratory airplane." In February of 1934 Jack Frye and Eddie Rickenbacker teamed up to set a nonstop cross-country record from Burbank, California to Newark, New Jersey, taking the last load of mail east before President Roosevelt canceled all commercial airmail contracts.

Later in 1934 the Department of Commerce and the Army Air Corps used the DC-1 to test the new Sperry automatic pilot which was linked to a radio compass and used for navigational purposes. Additional gasoline tanks were installed and the fuel capacity thus boosted from 500 to 1,600 gallons.

In 1935, two years after its maiden flight, the DC-1 was loaned by TWA to the National Aeronautics Association for an attempt to set new records for speed and distance and load. Within a three-day period, it smashed nineteen different records. Following this, Howard Hughes, millionaire sportsman and largest shareholder in TWA, planned a record-breaking round-the-world flight. He decided that the DC-1 was the airplane for the job and bought it from TWA in the summer of 1936. He modified it by again increasing the fuel capacity to give it the fantastic range of 6,000 miles and changed engines to give it more power. After exhaustive tests, however, Hughes chose the faster Lockheed 14 in which he later circled the globe in 91 hours.

Having bypassed the DC-1 for his round-the-world flight, Hughes sold it to an Englishman, Viscount Forbes, the Earl of Granard, in May 1937. By that time the DC-1 had accumulated 1,370 flying hours.

The DC-1's new owner wanted to fly the Atlantic, but Hughes talked him out of it. Instead, the viscount loaded it onto a freighter and had it shipped to England, where it was flown for about three months. The viscount soon tired of the airplane and sold it to a French company. Shortly thereafter, under rather mysterious circumstances, the DC-1 found itself in Spain just as the Spanish Civil War was drawing to a close.

By September of 1938 the Republican Government of Spain had purchased the famous airplane for L.A.P.E. (*Lineas Aeros Postales Españoles*). The shiny metal skin was painted dull brown, decorated with the Spanish registration, and put into regular service between Paris, Barcelona, and Albacete. Occasionally it was ordered on reconnaissance and communications missions for the Spanish Republican Army.

When Barcelona fell in March 1939, members of the Government escaped to Toulouse in the DC-1. It continued to fly wartime missions until the Republican forces collapsed in April 1939. Members of the defeated Government jumped into the DC-1 and headed for France. Nationalist Air Force fighter planes were alerted, but the DC-1 escaped undetected.

When the war was officially over, Nationalist pilots flew the One back to Madrid where it was handed over to the *Sociedad Anonima de Transportes Aeros,* later renamed Iberia. The camouflage paint was removed and the plane was officially christened "Negron" after a famous Nationalist pilot who had been killed in action. This time the DC-1 flew a regular passenger route connecting the major cities of Spain.

On a brisk December morning in 1940, "Negron" arrived at Malaga from Tetuan on schedule. The passengers were discharged, new ones took their places, the chocks removed from the wheels (it had no parking brakes) and the pilot, Captain Rudolfo Bay, readied for take-off. After the usual formalities of checking the engines, he lined up with the runway and poured on the power. Everything went fine until the plane left the ground. Suddenly the left engine failed as the pilot groped for altitude. He dropped the nose to attempt to regain lost flying speed, but the remaining engine would not carry the load. The pilot elected to try a landing straight ahead with his landing gear up. There was a sickening crash and, when the dust cleared, the DC-1 lay bent and broken just off the end of the runway. Passengers streamed out of the fuselage, followed by the crew. Not a person was hurt but the airplane was a complete wreck.

Since World War II had begun and few aircraft spare parts

were available, the airline decided to write the DC-1 off the books. Spanish mechanics towed the wreck to a corner of the field and salvaged what spare parts might be useful on other types of planes.

As an airplane, the DC-1 was a thing of the past. It had died in harness with an unmatched series of records as a memorial. But, strangely, this forefather of a long line of offspring, is still alive—in a way. Monks from the nearby Cathedral de Malaga needed a light but strong *andas*, or portable platform, which men would use to carry the image of the Blessed Virgin through the streets on religious holidays. Metal spars and the skin from the skeleton of the DC-1 were the answer. Thus, the grandfather of all Gooney Birds is still alive and doing a job that requires strength and dependability. Somehow, it seems right that the DC-1 was chosen to live on.

While the DC-1 had been setting records, the Douglas factory had tooled up for production of the DC-2, and the first of the new models rolled off the line and was accepted by TWA on May 14, 1934. Four days later its first scheduled run was made between Columbus, Ohio, and Newark, New Jersey. Other Two's quickly followed and were snatched up by eager airline buyers who realized that this was the airplane that could sell air travel to the public. One of the planes was sold to KLM, Royal Dutch Airlines. It was christened the "Uiver" and was promptly chosen to participate in the MacRobertson Trophy Race, better known as the London-to-Melbourne Derby.

Never in the history of aviation had there been a more impressive hour than that preceding the moment on October 20, 1934, when the Union Jack was dropped to signal the first airplane off in an air race from London, England, to Melbourne, Australia, in competition for the MacRobertson Trophy. Seven nations—Australia, England, Denmark, Holland, New Guinea, New Zealand, and the United States—were represented among the twenty planes in the race. The route was from London to Baghdad, then to Allahabad, Singapore, Darwin, and finally Charleville to Melbourne. Emergency stops could be made elsewhere without disqualification.

Imaginations had been fired. The roads for miles around the village of Mildenhall were choked with motorists, cyclists and hikers who had arisen at 4 A.M. to see the start of the race. They came from every direction, attracted by the group of heavily loaded airplanes of all sorts and configurations.

Beside the floodlit south hangar sat a big Boeing transport. Its mechanics busied themselves with last-minute details. One of its propellers moved briefly, stopped, moved again, and suddenly became a glistening disk while foot-long jets of orange flames belched from the exhausts.

Above the noise of the engines could be heard the monotone of a loudspeaker: "Clouds at 3,000 feet, visibility two miles, wind two-six-zero degrees at two-eight miles per hour . . ." and so on, with the weather being given for each large city along the 11,000-mile route to the land "down under."

The KLM DC-2 was moved onto the apron. Against a dawn background fit for the occasion—layer upon layer of jagged orange clouds faded into starlit purple—the DC-2, with its crew of K. D. Parmentier and J. J. Moll and three passengers, taxied along the front of the airport enclosure.

Probably what stirred more comment among the airport crowd than anything else was the fact that the KLM plane was taking along fare-paying passengers and mail. To KLM this was business, not exactly racing, and they were using this opportunity to test the last word in high-speed, high-performance transport planes.

Judging from the weather reports droning through the loudspeaker, the weather was not good over Europe. The few pilots who had chosen the great-circle route via Baghdad or Bucharest were less likely to have trouble than those flying by way of Marseilles or Rome. But this made little difference in the preparations. The crowd waited. The Lord Mayor of London, Sir Alfred Bower, was to start the first airplane off and the rest were to follow at 45-second intervals.

As the planes lined up abreast, the noise of the crowd was

smothered by the roar of the engines. Ten seconds to go. The first starter, James A. Mollison, opened the throttles of his twin-engined de Havilland *Comet.* "He's off!" the announcer blared. For a moment the *Comet* remained at the starting line, its propellers bright disks of light, then it moved, slowly gathered speed and lumbered off toward the sun. It was evident that the 260 gallons of fuel in the *Comet's* tanks was almost too much for Mollison's "Black Magic."

Next came the Boeing 247-D transport, piloted by Americans Roscoe Turner and Clyde Pangborn, which had rolled into position at the last moment. As the starter flicked his flag down, it roared over the sod field and rose slowly off the ground.

The third entry, another de Havilland *Comet,* being flown by Captain Cathcart-Jones and Kenneth Waller, had run about 200 yards when something went wrong. A jet of white flame belched from the left engine, causing the pilot to come to a screeching halt. Taxiing back into position, he tried again. This time he took off successfully, having lost only two minutes.

Entry Number Four, the de Havilland *Comet* piloted by Flight Lieutenant Charles W. A. Scott and Captain R. Campbell Black, took off. Fifth was the KLM DC-2. The big Douglas, its engines roaring confidently, was tucking its wheels up before it reached the boundary of the field. After the wheels disappeared into their wells, the plane rose noticeably, as if it carried no special load—quite a contrast to the seemingly overloaded aircraft that had preceded it.

Plane after plane became airborne, and as the last one disappeared, so did the crowd. They went home to tune in their wireless sets to follow the race to completion. The world waited for the first news, and when it came some of it was bad. A leaky radiator had forced one entry to land, out of the race, in the French countryside. Another was forced down at Boulogne, and still another near Paris. The hours ticked by.

The KLM transport, which many people had viewed skeptically because they didn't think it had a chance against the racing planes, experienced no in-flight difficulty and landed at Baghdad at 11:10 P.M. Three hours later Roscoe Turner's

Boeing also landed at Baghdad and left again for Karachi after
only a 30-minute gas stop. Other aircraft came in at intervals,
some of them having had to stop two or three times for gas
and oil. News of other planes drifted to the crew of the KLM
DC-2, Parmentier and Moll, and it wasn't cheerful news. Several
entries had crashed, others had detoured because of bad
weather, and still others had had mechanical trouble which
they could not rectify.

While the others were having their troubles, the DC-2 landed
at Jask, Karachi, and then Allahabad, leaving Allahabad after
an hour's fuel stop. There was no doubt that it was pushing
the leaders, but anything could happen in a race of this kind.
The Dutchmen were running true to their preannounced
schedule—just as a good airline should. They even returned to
Allahabad to pick up a strayed passenger!

Captain Scott, flying a *Comet*, was the first to reach Australia,
and everyone was certain that he had the race cinched.
Parmentier and Moll announced that they were going all out
to get Scott, but no one thought the lumbering Douglas had
a chance.

The DC-2 reached Batavia as Roscoe Turner's Boeing passed
Rangoon, and the second *Comet*, flown by Mollison, reached
Allahabad. All the other planes still in the race were behind
the two *Comets*, the Douglas, and the Boeing.

Then came the big news. Scott had landed at Darwin with
an elapsed time of two days four and a half hours—the last two
and a half hours on one engine! Everyone wanted to know if
it would be possible to repair the engine in time to finish, or
would Scott try to go the rest of the way on one engine.

The intrepid Scott elected to try it on one engine. Averaging
only 154 miles an hour, he reached Charleville, Australia. The
DC-2 was a thousand miles behind him, followed closely by
the Boeing. Scott left Charleville and headed for Melbourne.

Three hours later the DC-2 landed at Charleville, took on
gas, exchanged mail, and left for its final destination some seven
hours after the *Comet*. After leaving Charleville, the KLM
crew had to make a forced landing at night on a race track at

Albury because of faulty navigation. In the meantime the Boeing was on its way to Charleville. The Dutch pilots weren't concerned, however. With the Boeing still 1,300 miles away, the Douglas seemed to be in second place. A night take-off might have been possible but the pilots decided to wait until daylight.

Anxious people all over the world wondered who would win second place. The final result is history. The Dutch entry took off from the race track with ease the next morning, just as it was able to do years later in the jungles of the South Pacific islands. The Douglas DC-2 landed at Melbourne 71 hours and 28 minutes after leaving Mildenhall, having flown at an average speed of 173 miles per hour (including ground time). In an 11,000-mile race it had placed second to a souped-up fighter plane which had won only because the pilot took the desperate chance of flying his plane on one engine. The DC-2 had had no trouble, the mail was delivered, and the three passengers stepped nonchalantly off the airplane looking refreshed and relaxed. This performance proved that dependability, service, comfort, and speed could all be built into one airplane. The race made the name "Douglas" world famous.

After the race of 1934, the DC-2 became the sensation of the aviation industry. It seemed incredible that a transport plane, matched against the best racing aircraft of the day, could make such a magnificent showing. The aviation press, instead of concentrating on the winner, directed its attention to the new DC transport. The "Douglas" promised to revolutionize air transportation.

The world's airlines, such as they were, had showed little official interest in the race, yet they soon began showering the Douglas factory with orders. TWA ordered more DC-2s; Eddie Rickenbacker ordered fourteen for his Eastern Airlines. Almost every major airline, American or foreign, wanted DC-2s, or at least made inquiries.

As the DC-2s rolled out of the Santa Monica factory, an era of intense competition began among the airlines. TWA seemed to be capturing the coast-to-coast air-travel business. As air travelers flocked to TWA to try the new Douglas planes, United Airlines found that its Boeing 247s were getting less and less popular. Other airlines still flying the older Ford trimotors, *Condors,* Fokkers and Stinsons realized they had better join the race for newer and better equipment.

As the months passed, airlines that had once been cautious about getting in on the ground floor with a new airplane were clamoring for the new bird. Douglas had to continually expand production facilities to meet the demand. Donald Douglas had built a better airplane and the world was beating a path to his door.

Foreign governments came to look and buy. A licensing agreement was made in 1934 with the Nakajima Aircraft Company to build DC-2s. Five airframes were purchased and assembled in Japan and one complete DC-2 was bought in Canada. All six planes were later used in airline service. The Russians made a copy of the DC-2 with slightly modified wing and tail contours and labeled it the ANT-35. It was powered by Gnome-Rhone M-85 engines.

With the DC-2's introduction of new luxury to air travelers, airline executives began to think about sleeper airplanes for the coast-to-coast journey. American Airlines was first to introduce the idea with its Curtiss *Condor* biplane sleeper in 1934. It became popular but it wasn't fast enough. Airline operators wanted a bigger, faster airplane that could leave New York at sundown, make the coast-to-coast flight overnight, and land in California the following morning. Passengers wanted to be able to stretch out in Pullmanlike berths instead of trying to catnap in the reclining seats of dayliners.

Douglas, alert to the demands of his fast-growing list of customers, set his engineers to work. William Littlewood, chief engineer for American Airlines, developed a set of specifications. American Airlines knew that the DC-2 was the best plane built up to that time for airline use, but the executives also knew that no airline could carry a big enough payload on each trip to make a substantial profit.

The Littlewood specifications called for increasing the

passenger capacity from 14 to 21. The requirement was translated into sketches by Douglas engineers, and struck the fine balance that all airlines engineers strive for in speed, gross weight, power, payload, space and wing area.

As they stretched the fuselage of the DC-2 to make room for more passengers and comfortable berths, they found they had created a brand-new airplane—the DC-3.

The plane that saved the airlines

2

It was the first airplane . . . that could make money just by hauling passengers.

—C. R. SMITH
President, American Airlines

WHILE DOUGLAS EMPLOYEES were putting the finishing touches on DC-2 Number 185, the first DC-3 rolled out on the ramp beside it. Others quickly followed and the new version created quite a sensation as the top airline brass flocked to Santa Monica to see its first flight on the thirty-second anniversary of the Wright brothers' epic flight—December 17, 1935. The airline officials learned that the DC-3 was being produced in several models. A 21-passenger day-plane, 14-passenger luxury *Skysleeper*, and a luxurious club-car-of-the-air, the 14-passenger *Skylounge*, were available. They found that the new "Three" flew higher, faster, and had more gadgets on it for passenger safety and comfort than the DC-2. In short, they learned that this was the ultimate in aircraft and that they had better get their names on order blanks if they wanted airplanes in the near future. They ordered, and with the DC-3 came a new era for the air traveler. American Airlines placed the first quantity order and became the first airline in the world to put the new plane into service. The date was June 25, 1936, a day that marked the end of profitless airline flying.

A week later, on July 1, 1936—exactly three years to a day since the DC-1 had made its first flight—Donald W. Douglas stood in the office of the President of the United States to receive aviation's coveted Collier Trophy for having developed "the most outstanding twin-engined transport plane."

"This airplane," President Roosevelt said, "by reason of its high speed, economy, and quiet passenger comfort has been generally adopted by transport lines throughout the United States. Its merit has been further recognized by its adoption abroad and its influence on foreign design is already apparent."

No longer was the hapless passenger forced to balance his box lunch on his knees while munching a cold sandwich or an apple. No longer would he suffer from deafness, gastric disturbances, cold feet, and lack of sleep. Now chic stewardesses brought handy trays containing full course meals from soup to nuts. And the meals were free. Between meals the stewardesses served hot bouillon or coffee and cookies. They chatted with the passengers, pointed out interesting places along the route and did everything possible to make their charges happy.

By the end of 1936, most of the nation's airlines had standardized on the DC-3 or were planning to convert to it. A new record had been set: a million passengers had boarded the scheduled airliners for the first time. The American public, because of the influence of this new airplane, was slowly becoming airminded. In the next three years the two million passenger mark would be passed.

Slowly, the airlines found that the enlarged version of the

DC-2 spelled the difference between profit and loss and removed what was the greatest danger in commercial flying of the time—the danger of the airline's going broke. It was at this time that C. R. Smith, president of American Airlines, said that the DC-3 "was the first airplane in the world that could make money just by hauling passengers."

The airlines then took on a new kind of profit-making complexion never before possible. Maine lobsters, which previously had been placed in bulky containers and packed in several layers of ice to prevent spoilage on long rail journeys, were now shipped fast in lightweight containers across the country in half a day. People on the West Coast and in the South who had never tasted Maine lobster found they could enjoy it often, and thus there was little increase in price. Orchid growers were able to ship fresh flowers to any part of the United States by air. Fruits, vegetables, and even animals were flown in the DC airplane. It was then that the railroads began to take notice. Their business was beginning to hurt because airplanes could haul freight over long distances at faster speeds on regular schedules and do it safely. A whole new industry had been born!

With each hour in the air, the pilots grew more experienced in the new all-metal planes. These planes were comparatively easy to fly, and did not tax the physical stamina of the pilots as had the old planes. Before too many years had passed, there were pilots who had accumulated great amounts of flying time. When a man reached a certain point in his flying career he became a "Million Miler."

Captain Charles W. Meyers, a retired Eastern Airlines pilot, was one of these Million Milers. He, like hundreds of other pilots who became Million Milers, has a wealth of stories to tell about the old DC-3.

"During my years with Eastern I put about 9,000 hours in DC airplanes," Meyers relates. "Other than occasional minor difficulties, I had no serious mechanical failures. This, to me, points out the fine engineering that went into Douglas airplanes. We on the airlines should know. We flew them through thunderstorms, ice, sleet, hail, and hurricanes. As far as I know, none were lost because of mechanical or structural failure. At times we thought the big wings might buckle in a storm because we could actually see them wiggle. But this, as far as I know, never happened. They were sturdy, to say the least.

"The DC-3 was, in my opinion, the steppingstone for pilots from the Ford and Stinson trimotors, the *Condors* and Boeings to the modern airliner. It was just the schooling and transition airplane we needed for the complicated jet airplanes of today.

"We who flew the DC-3 had complete confidence in it. I might relate one incident that will serve to show how we got that confidence.

"I had left Atlanta one night headed for Chicago, with scheduled stops at Chattanooga, Nashville, and Louisville. Out of Atlanta the weather in front of us was anything but the best. Chattanooga, Nashville, and Louisville were socked in, and Atlanta went down to zero right after take-off. Over Chattanooga we rammed into a cold front full of wet snow and ice. We were at 5,000 feet when one engine began to lose power because of an iced-up carburetor. I turned on the carburetor heat control but it simply wouldn't melt the ice. The power dropped off so rapidly that I knew I had to do something fast.

"My copilot, Hank Freese, had been a barnstormer back in the early days just as I had been. I reminded him of the days when we were often bothered with ice and said, 'Hank, lean it out until it backfires, like we used to do.' Hank pulled back the mixture control until the engine backfired several times and blew the slushy ice out of the carburetor.

"About this time," continued Meyers, "we hit the front that was causing all this foul weather. We were kicked upstairs, at higher altitude. What I mean is this: We hit a bad updraft that threw us from 5,000 feet up to 13,000 in nothing flat. Then we shot back down, fast, then on up to 10,000 and finally back to 5,000 feet again. Talk about being busy! All that concerned me was keeping my air speed within the safety mark and keeping the bird straight and level. I wasn't particularly concerned how high the updrafts took us, but I would have worried some if it had started tossing us down below the 5,000-foot mark.

"While we were jockeying up and down in the dark sky, the second engine carburetor froze up and we had to blow out the ice like we had in the first one. There is always a danger of catching fire when you resort to this method of deicing a carburetor, but when the ice is too heavy for the heat control to melt you don't have much choice. Besides, we had fire extinguishers in the engines that could be released if an engine caught fire.

"Chattanooga, Nashville and Louisville were all socked in. The weather was so bad in those places we couldn't even think about landing. By this time the wings, propellers, and tail surfaces were loaded with ice and we were carrying about all the power the engines would stand to keep the bird in the air. Every once in a while the ice would break loose from the propellers and crash against the side of the airplane. I know the passengers were wondering what was going on outside, and I am sure they were a bit concerned. For certain, I was!

"The nearest place I figured we could put the big plane down was Indianapolis. I checked the weather there and it was bad. When you're flying a route like this you have to figure the odds in every case. I had already passed over three landing places and wasn't overloaded with fuel, by any means. Sooner or later I had to set down somewhere and not endanger the lives of the people for whom I was responsible. Besides, I cared a little for my own neck, too.

"Stumbling around in the darkness with poor radio reception, we finally found the Indianapolis radio range station and circled for a clearance. I tried a landing but found that my windshield was so covered with ice that I couldn't see ahead. I pulled back up, took the hand fire extinguisher and slammed it against the left corner windshield and broke it.

The cold air rushed in and chilled my face, momentarily blinding me, but at least I could see the runway to make my next approach. Looking cockeyed out of the corner glass, I finally got the bird on the ground.

"On the ramp my copilot and I looked the bird over. There were about two inches of ice on the wings, tail and nose, and it was solid. From that moment on, Hank Freese and I were convinced that we were flying the only airplane in the world that could do what that airplane did for us that night. Believe me, any time you can take an airplane, load it with a ton or more of ice, plus a load of passengers, baggage and mail, fly solid instruments from Atlanta to Indianapolis and do it all with partial or intermittent power, that's the airplane for me. I think I can speak for all the old DC-3 pilots—and there are lots of them floating around, probably still flying the same old bird—when I say that all of us have deep respect for the old girl. It does my heart good to see them still flying confidently along the feeder airways today. I'm sure they will never wear out."

While the airlines were having a heyday with their new airplane and bursting with happiness that the new DC was bringing them out of the red into the black, war clouds loomed on the horizon. A mustached, hysterical former paper hanger named Adolf Hitler was screaming his defiance to the world. Hitler was telling the German people that it was time for the master race to dominate the world.

Germany had been shorn of military aircraft after World War I and was supposedly at the bottom of the heap with regard to trained pilots and airplane mechanics. But under Hitler's leadership, the Third Reich had secretly grown in military air strength. Hundreds of pilots and crewmen had been trained in gliders and "commercial" aircraft. As a result, Germany's airlines grew, and by 1939 Germany had a network of airlines linking the Fatherland with Africa, the Middle East, and South America. Also, German-dominated airlines stretched the length and breadth of South America.

There was little question in the minds of the men in the

State Department that Germany intended to turn its commercial air domination to military advantage. A vital air lifeline—the 2,660-mile stretch running from Lima, Peru, to Rio de Janeiro, Brazil—was being spanned daily by a German airline. This route was slowly expanded north through Ecuador to Colombia and south to Uruguay, Paraguay, and Argentina. By 1939 the transcontinental thread had become an economic chain.

In Brazil the Nazi syndicate had built landing fields on the strategic shoulder jutting out into the Atlantic where bombers and troops could be landed from Africa. Innocent-appearing merchant vessels could, and did, reconnoiter the ocean and guide German U-boats to their prey. In addition, these same innocent-looking transport ships warned blockade-running Axis merchantmen of the presence of Allied warships. It was an ideal setup for Hitler. The comprehensive planning and attention to detail placed him in a position to rush in bombers and troop planes to take advantage of the political vacuum caused by a revolution in any South American country.

The best part of the plan, from Hitler's viewpoint, was that it threw a monkey wrench into the war plans of the United States. America couldn't make a decision to strike east or west so long as there was the danger of enemy bombers coming from the south to blast the locks of the Panama Canal, attack Caribbean bases, or bomb American cities.

The United States did have a sword, however, with which to lop off Hitler's hold on South America at a single stroke. If the sale of gasoline to South America were stopped, not a single Axis plane could take off. But the sword was double-edged. If it were used without a declaration of war, there was the danger of cutting the bonds of friendship with South America which was a vital part of U. S. anti-Nazi strategy.

The Germans had used the same foresight in this maneuver that characterized all their war plans. While the U. S. had kept its activities strictly on a commercial basis, Germany had been playing Santa Claus with the small struggling nations of South America. The airlines had been established there by the Germans without regard to cost or profit; and passengers and freight were benevolently flown over the entire continent at constant loss. The countries slowly became dependent upon the German airlines and took ever-increasing advantage of the low fares and fairly dependable service.

The menace grew daily. As Hitler made his moves, one by one, in Europe, tons of airplane spare parts began to flow into the strategic shoulder of Brazil. Condor Airlines had established some 3,000 miles of air routes where traffic possibilities were practically nonexistent. But the strategic import was obvious to our trained observers. At the same time, Lufthansa-Peru and Sedta Airlines increased their networks, and Lati, an Italian transoceanic airline, doubled its schedules, thus providing an invaluable channel for inter-Axis diplomatic mail, wireless transmitting sets, and Axis agents.

The German menace, which comprised some 33,000 miles of air routes by the time war was declared against Great Britain in September of 1939, had to be stopped quickly. Washington strategists decided to duplicate all the German air routes and have them flown by American crews and planes. Since the German airlines were popular, as well as cheap, it meant that superior service would have to be provided by U. S. airlines in order to make the plan economically feasible.

Pan-American Airways was the obvious organization to tackle the enormous task. Having started operations in Latin America in 1927, it had rounded out a system of trunk airlines linking all the capitals of South America with the United States and, in so doing, it had won the confidence of all the Latin American governments. Pan-American chose the DC-2s and DC-3s as her weapons. Nineteen airplanes were assigned to the Eastern Division, while Panagra, the name of the South American west coast system, was boosted to 14 airplanes. The strategy was to cut flying time, stress safety,

and operate on-the-minute schedules and thus attempt to
drive the Axis operation out of business by sheer efficiency
of operation.

Panagra duplicated Sedta's routes early in 1941, and was
shortly carrying three times the German company's volume
of freight and passengers. Pan-American increased its schedules between Buenos Aires, Argentina, and Santiago, Chile,
and paralleled Condor's operations over the Andes. At the
same time, in the vital Colombia area, Panagra, which
owned 80 per cent of the stock, bought up the contracts of
all the German employees of Scadta and reorganized it into
a strong, national company called Avianca. Then Panagra
purchased a new line which discharged German employees
had organized, and thus completely terminated all Axis
influence in the proximity of the Canal Zone.

Panagra increased the DC-3 service on the trunk lines
running north and south, making it possible for Peru to cancel Lufthansa's permits and expropriate that company's
equipment when the Germans sabotaged interned ships in
the harbor of Callao. One after another the Latin countries
were able to cancel or expropriate the German airlines for
cause. When Washington, in agreement with the Brazilian
Government, shut off Condor's gasoline supplies, that most
important of German airlines was put out of business without any inconvenience to the Brazilian public. When the
Japanese bombed Pearl Harbor on December 7, 1941, all
that remained of Lufthansa's South American air empire was
a short seventy-mile stretch over the Andes. This route
ceased operation the same week.

When this undeclared airline war had started, the Axis-
owned or controlled airlines in South America were operating some 33,000 air-route miles, whereas Pan-American,
with its affiliated companies, had only 18,460 miles. A week
after Pearl Harbor the Pan-American system had expanded
to some 59,000 route miles.

What makes this story significant is the fact that the Axis
could not have been squeezed out of South America if-

American airplanes had not been available in sufficient quantity. With the DC-2s and DC-3s, Pan-American not only made it possible for the United States Government to drive out the Axis menace without inconvenience to its southern neighbors, but provided them with a better service in the bargain. It was the Gooney Bird that won the airline war against the Axis in South America before the real war ever started.

The DC is drafted

3

I came to admire this machine which could lift virtually any load strapped to its back and carry it anywhere in any weather, safely and dependably. The C-47 groaned, it protested, it rattled, it leaked oil, it ran hot, it ran cold, it ran rough, it staggered along on hot days and scared you half to death, its wings flexed and twisted in a horrifying manner, it sank back to earth with a great sigh of relief—but it flew and it flew and it flew.

—Len Morgan
The Douglas DC-3

THE SCENE in the Munitions Building where the top brass of the War Department met to discuss the need for rapid development of the United States aviation industry was tense. Although the DC-2 had been accepted and had proven itself to the civilian airlines, there was skepticism regarding its military use. Ground generals wondered what real value, if any, airplanes would have in the war that seemed inevitable.

In the midst of the Depression, Congress had taken a dim view of huge appropriations for military aircraft. Each airplane that was purchased, or was being considered for inclusion in the military air inventory, had to be completely justified. Those who remembered the small part that the airplane had played in World War I were convinced that the next war—if there was one—would still be fought in the trenches.

The Secretary of War appointed a board to determine the types of aircraft needed by the Army and to make recommendations for future requirements of the nation's stepchild air arm. The board believed, and rightly so, that improvements in airplane design always came about through the competition of aircraft manufacturers. Speed, efficiency, and safety of flight were among the topmost considerations in determining which planes would be taken into the U. S. Army Air Corps. The board insisted that all new technical developments should be promptly and thoroughly tested by the Army Air Corps. Thus it was that attention was directed toward the revolutionary Douglas transport planes. Just as there was a growing need for transporting civilians across the country, it was logical to assume that the Army would need planes to transport troops and equipment if war should come.

By 1938, no other company had produced an airplane, or even a design, to match the DC transports. The Defense Board reasoned that the Douglas company might be able to turn out slightly modified versions in quantity and still maintain the highest quality, therefore the board suggested that the Chief of Staff of the Army Air Corps should study the procurement of Douglas transports without delay.

Air Corps experts examined the DC design and pored over the reports of the exhaustive tests made on the DC-1 and the DC-2 by TWA. The Air Corps had borrowed the DC-1 briefly from TWA to test the Sperry autopilot, and Air Corps engineers had installed 1,600-gallon fuel tanks which tripled the DC's range.

A report was then submitted to the Chief of Staff of the

Army Air Corps, General Benjamin D. Foulois. This report recommended that the DC design be modified and that several prototypes be procured for tests under simulated battle conditions.

While the United States Army Air Corps was considering the possible adoption of the DC-2 as a standard military transport, four of the early civilian models had found their way to Spain to serve on the side of the Loyalists during the Spanish Civil War.

As a regular procedure, the hard-pressed Loyalists loaded the 14-passenger DC-2s with thirty or more people and repeatedly outran the fighters of the Germans and Italians. Francisco Batet, a flight mechanic on a Loyalist DC-2, related several stories about the airplane, and told of its first taste of war:

"Throughout the thirty months of the war our four Douglas transports were never out of service, and during that time they were never housed in hangars. We always operated from provisional fields either by the seashore or in the mountains. Furthermore, we flew them both night and day, and all during the war we subjected them to punishment no other airplane could have withstood. They gave us courage. They proved that they would not let us down on any occasion.

"Once a crew was pursued by a squadron of Fiat fighters on the Estremadura front. Because of the greater speed of the Douglas, the Fiats soon fell behind.

"When we were transferred to Valencia we accomplished, with the DC-2s, 182 liaison flights between Valencia and Santander in a straight line which crossed 311 miles of enemy territory. We did this without fighter protection and without armament, and we were always extremely overloaded. During these operations we were pursued eight times, but the Fiats never caught us or even annoyed us seriously.

"During May 1937, we transferred some troops from

Valencia to Tarragona. With enough gasoline for only an hour and a half of flying time, we carried thirty-five men with rifles in each plane on each trip. On one of those flights the pilot of our plane didn't realize that the airfield at Tarragona had recently been bombed. After he was already on the ground he learned too late that the plane was heading for a huge hole made by a bomb. The left wheel dropped into the hole with a sickening crunch and the wing on that side was slammed against the ground. The ground crews dragged the plane out of the hole, back to solid ground; then the pilot and crew made an inspection to determine the extent of the damage. Much to their dismay, the wing was bent upward about four meters from its connection with the fuselage.

"While the crew continued to examine the airplane, looking at it with both sorrow and disgust, someone shouted that enemy planes were approaching the airfield. The pilot yelled for his crew to board the crippled DC-2. He flipped the switches, the engines roared, and with complete disregard for the horribly bent wing, they took off as if nothing had happened.

"On the ground at Valencia, they continued the aircraft inspection. The flight had seemingly been impossible, yet the airplane limped in safely. It was later ascertained that the upper surface of the left wing formed an angle of seventeen degrees!

"On another occasion a box of ammunition exploded beside one of the DC-2s, killing three men and destroying half the fuselage between the entrance door and the tail. The gaping hole had so distorted the fuselage that a glance indicated the plane might never fly again. Working out in the open at the provisional field where maintenance facilities were practically nonexistent, the crews patched the torn fuselage. When it was completed, the pilot gave it a test flight. He reported that the old plane flew as it always had.

"We began the war with four Douglas transports. Each one flew more than 2,000 hours during the conflict. They were finally surrendered to Franco, old and with many scars, but they were covered with glory and in good condition."

Major General Benjamin D. Foulois, long-time pioneer in aviation, agreed with the findings of the board that transport airplanes selected for the Air Corps should be selected "off the shelf" from existing standard commercial types. In one respect, however, Foulois disagreed with the board's findings. He did not agree that an airplane equipped to carry passengers could also carry bulky cargo and equipment.

Another consideration argued by Foulois was that the Army had pushed the development of a special military cargo airplane which was to be delivered in August 1934 by the Fairchild Corporation. He believed it might be good enough to be adopted as the standard military air transport.

The Fairchild plane was finally delivered, but soon developed some aerodynamic "bugs" and was grounded. However, the original concept and specifications were still considered valid. Based on the Fairchild plans, Foulois's staff announced a requirement for a cargo plane whose tactical mission would be to transport military matériel and troops to front-line airdromes and to evacuate sick and wounded in case of war. Specifically, bids were invited from the aircraft industry to supply the Army with an airplane that could haul a payload of 3,000 pounds; have a cruising speed of 125 miles per hour, a high speed of 150 miles per hour, and a range of 500 miles while doing at least 125 miles per hour. The bid invitation further stated that the plane's landing speed could not exceed 60 miles an hour.

The specifications were sent to the various aircraft companies and several manufacturers put their engineers to work to see what could be developed. Douglas, already tooled up for the DC-2s, was among the first to submit a bid. Based on an order for twenty, Douglas told the War Department that he could produce them for $61,775 each, plus $20,500 for the two engines. That made the Douglas bid $82,275 per airplane.

After all the bids were in, the Air Corps flight-tested the various models entered, including the DC-2. The Douglas entry received an aggregate score of 786 points and placed first. The Fairchild Company placed second with 599.7 points. When the test results were sent to Washington, the contracting officer recommended that the contract be awarded to Douglas even though he noted that the aircraft requirements program for 1936 approved by Congress, called for thirty-six cargo aircraft of the *single*-engine type.

When the report reached General Foulois's desk, he sought an opinion from the Judge Advocate General. Could thirty-six *twin*-engine transports be procured or must only single-engine planes be ordered? He was advised that a purchase of eighteen *twin*-engine cargo airplanes was authorized but no more. The contract was drawn up and the new Air Corps plane was designated the C-33.

When the first C-33s rolled off the production line, performance data showed that this version of the DC-2 could carry a useful load of 6,320 pounds, fly at 171 miles per hour, and cover a distance of 916 miles. Having been modified to meet the Army's needs, many innovations were incorporated into the C-33. Two loading methods were provided: In one, a hoist was attached to a tripod on top of the fuselage and cargo was lifted into the cabin by a winch permanently attached to the forward bulkhead. In the other, tracks were used and the material was drawn into the cabin by a system of pulleys and cables. Other changes were made to allow the C-33 to carry nine standard Air Corps litters or twelve commercial-type passenger chairs. All specifications were not only met but exceeded.

It wasn't long, however, before someone decided to change the specifications again. In January 1935 the Commanding General of the Air Corps General Headquarters (GHQ) decided he needed a personal plane. The equipment, besides the usual reclining chairs, was to include desks, filing cabinets, and other office facilities. Since the DC-2 (not the C-33) had recently undergone flight tests at Wright Field, Ohio, it was reasoned that the DC-2 could serve the purpose with only minor cabin modifications.

But the Secretary of War had other ideas. He had approved specifications for an airplane which would carry a payload of 3,600 pounds or 18 passengers. The commercial DC-2 could carry only 2,500 pounds or 10 passengers. This automatically precluded the procurement of the DC-2 and all other standard commercial types then in production.

Faced with this decision, General Foulois suggested that the minimum specifications be reduced to allow the DC-2 to fall within those limits. A compromise was finally reached and a contract negotiated with Douglas for one 14-passenger DC-2 which was designated the XC-32. An order for twenty-four C-32As quickly followed. In January 1936 two more were ordered under slightly different specifications, and these were called C-34s.

Months passed while the Army tested its new transports extensively. In the meantime, Douglas engineers had designed the DC-3 to meet new airline specifications. The Air Corps promptly asked for changes in specifications, and one C-33 with a DC-3 tail was constructed and designated the C-38. The tests proved successful and an order for thirty-five C-39s was placed which were DC-2s with a DC-3 tail modified inside for carrying cargo.

As was often the case in the days before the attack on Pearl Harbor, aircraft development and procurement were controlled to a great extent by men who had never flown and who were not even remotely acquainted with aerodynamics or the capabilities of airplanes. Army officers with no knowledge of flight characteristics insisted that the loading door on the new C-39 should be made wider to accommodate a 75-mm. field piece. Another officer insisted that the floor be rebuilt so it would remain level while the airplane was on the ground. Still another believed that the floor-boards should be covered with a certain type of sandpaper-like material so paratroopers wouldn't slip as they went out the door. To attempt to satisfy all the suggestions, single purchases were made of a C-41, C-41A, and C-42.

While the idea of nonflying officers making suggestions did not appeal to the pilots responsible for procuring and testing the planes, they had to admit that many of the suggestions proved worthy of adoption. The sandpaper idea, for example, was excellent. Strips of tough, gritty material were installed on the floor and were used throughout the war. To this day the material is still being used in military C-47s.

Patient Douglas engineers took modification requests, studied them and were able to make most of the changes requested and often were able to improve on the ideas submitted. After the C-39 was modified, it *could* carry the 75-mm. cannon, drop men and supplies, carry litter patients, and serve as an airborne office. Furthermore, the change-over to carry these varying types of load could be made in minutes.

During this period of modification so many changes were made inside and out that the Army designated the final product the C-47. However, there were others called the C-48, C-49, C-50, C-51, C-52, C-53, and C-68. Of these, only the C-49 and C-53 were produced in quantity. The only difference between the C-47 and these two was that the C-49 was the *Skysleeper* version of the DC-3 which was easily adapted into a comfortable air evacuation airplane. The C-53 was the paratroop version. After the war a plushed-up version of the C-47 became the C-117 and one Super DC-3, designated the YC-129, was purchased by the Air Force.

With all the numbers used to designate its models, the Air Corps settled on the C-47 to be produced in great quantity. It was soon found that the C-47 could be produced with all the other modifications built into it at the factory. Besides, it was easier to mass-produce one model of an airplane than four or five which were *almost* alike.

While the U. S. Army's air arm was struggling mightily to convince a disinterested Congress that the nation needed planes for defense, the Germans proved what Billy Mitchell had preached for fifteen years before his death. The airplane *could* be the most potent weapon ever devised if properly employed. The Germans blitzed their way into Norway and the Low Countries. Dive bombers preceded troop transports which disgorged parachute troops into carefully chosen areas to pioneer the maneuver known as "vertical envelopment."

Stimulated by the success of the Germans, the United States Army organized a parachute platoon for experimental purposes in early 1940. By September the War Department ordered the platoon built up to battalion strength. Later more battalions were organized, and by December 1941, the four battalions had become regiments which formed the nucleus of the Army's first two airborne divisions.

Until November 1941, however, the Army Air Forces had never been capable of dropping more than one company at a time. The reason was simple—there weren't enough transport planes to take care of the sudden expansion of airborne units.

As early as February 1933, the Army Air Corps had set up air transport units to fly air freight between the several matériel depots across the nation. These units grew slowly and when war began in Europe in 1939 there was only one transport group of four squadrons of nine or ten airplanes each. In addition to these, the Air Corps had fifty transports, assigned to Air Corps tactical units, which transported ground maintenance personnel and supplies on maneuvers. On these maneuvers the transports were usually pooled in temporary organizations.

It was ironic that the United States Army Air Corps had pioneered in the use of air transports beginning in 1931, and yet had not organized them into permanent units. Driven by the sudden urgent need for fighters and bombers, and influenced by a belief that transports could always be bought off the shelf, the Air Corps placed almost no new orders for any type of transport airplane in 1939 or the first half of 1940. In June 1940, however, this policy was abruptly

changed. It was realized that the United States Army had
more than a hundred aging transports and that new ones
could not be bought off the shelf as had been supposed.
Army planners now wanted 11,802 transports to support the
nation's expanding military organization, but from June to
December of 1940 only five planes had been delivered. At
the end of 1940 the Army had an anemic total of 122 transports, mostly obsolete C-33s and C-39s. During 1941 only
133 more were delivered.

Considering these statistics, it is not difficult to explain
why the Army Air Corps objected when Fort Benning asked
for thirty-nine airplanes for paratroop training for the November 1941 maneuvers.

By December 1941, the Air Corps was faced with a serious problem. Deliveries were still small and the airplanes in
the inventory were already obsolescent. To make up the
shortage in case of war a plan was drawn up whereby the
airlines would lend the Government a number of planes.
Their experienced flight crews, their knowledge of air routes,
and their excellent airplanes and supporting equipment thus
provided a reserve air fleet that would prove invaluable. The
airlines, under this plan, would be asked to provide transportation of men and supplies for the armed services to all parts
of the world. They would also train military men in airline
operation and convert airline company shops into
modification and repair facilities. The plan was accepted by
the entire airline industry. It was to be put into operation
sooner than anyone would have believed possible.

On Sunday morning, December 7, 1941, an American Airlines DC-3, lumbering along on the coast-to-coast run, was
approaching Phoenix, Arizona. The passenger list included a
well-known movie star, several prominent businessmen en
route to their respective homes in California after confer-
ences in Washington, and a few assorted passengers who
were happy to be aboard because they had been forced to
book passage weeks in advance in order to get a seat. In the

cockpit the two pilots relaxed comfortably, one listening to the company radio and the other flying and maintaining a "listening watch" on the CAA radio range frequency. Without warning of what was coming, an excited voice on the Phoenix frequency shouted, "American Twenty-One, this is Phoenix Radio. Plan A! Plan A!"

That's all there was to the message. It was simple but its meaning was electrifying. This message, containing one word and one letter of the alphabet was a code message that meant that war had come. Within a few minutes after the word of the Japanese attack on Pearl Harbor, similar coded messages were flashed to every passenger plane plying the nation's airways. The airlines were at war and were the first commercial enterprise to realize it. This was part of the prearranged airline mobilization plan made with the military. It was perhaps prophetic that the crew of a DC-3 would be among the first to know of World War II. What no one knew on that fateful day, however, was the role that the faithful DC-3 was to play in the four-year drama that lay ahead. Certainly no one would have ever bet that the lumbering, ungainly DC-3 would be called one of the pieces of equipment that won the war by a general who would one day be the President of the United States.

The Gooney Bird goes to war

4

... four other pieces of equipment that most senior officers came to regard as among the most vital to our success in Africa and Europe were the bulldozer, the jeep, the 2½-ton truck, and the C-47 airplane. Curiously, none of these is designed for combat.

—Dwight D. Eisenhower
Crusade in Europe

During World War II, more than five million men and women wore the uniform of one of the nation's armed forces. There were few who did not depend to some extent at some time upon the military versions of the DC airplane. These planes carried ammunition, gasoline, food, and medical supplies to the fighting men at the front; they carried out the wounded to behind-the-lines hospitals; they carried tired combat crews to rest areas in Australia and New Zealand, and brought fresh milk and eggs back to the Pacific islands on return trips; they carried paratroopers and dropped hundreds of them behind the enemy lines; they flew for the partisans in Yugoslavia and for the chetniks of Mihajlovic; they became bombers, and at least one became a fighter plane with a victory to its credit. In fact, it would be impossible to mention all the jobs the reliable Gooney Bird performed. It became a legend. Wherever it flew its familiar shape and sound could be recognized.

One of the first war areas to test the real capability of the C-47 was the Pacific theater, where almost any flight to anywhere was over water and the distances were great. There were few radio facilities to guide the pilots from one point to another, and the Gooney Birds were so slow that unless the navigators stayed alert, a strong crosswind in flight could blow them far off course.

One could not say that taking one island from the Japanese was exactly like taking another. Some of the islands were coral atolls where there was little undergrowth; others contained many kinds of vegetation and terrain. And there were islands covered with dense jungle undergrowth that the enemy clung to tenaciously and that gave the defenders an advantage. Such was Guadalcanal.

Despite their serious losses in the naval battles of Midway and the Coral Sea, the Japanese had succeeded in bringing reinforcements to the island of Guadalcanal until it seemed they had enough troops there to force the bedraggled U. S. Marines off the island. The enemy advantage both in the air and on the sea was not only numerical superiority but also lay in his much closer supply bases. Many of his forward bases were in the Solomon Islands group to which Guadalcanal belonged.

American forward bases were at least a thousand miles distant and the nearest supporting air base to the south was a crude, matted strip cut among the hills and jungles 640 miles away in the New Hebrides—Espíritu Santo Island.

However, the American troops still retained possession of

Henderson airfield on Guadalcanal. Here a makeshift force composed of approximately seventy Army and Marine aircraft operated in spite of day and night enemy air raids. Nightly shellfire from Japanese cruisers zeroed in on Henderson's strip which represented the only offensive base for attacks against enemy naval and air forces, as well as providing the launching point for air support of American ground forces.

Some four thousand Army reinforcements and ground force supplies had recently been landed on the island by the Navy, whose primary task was to support the embattled ground forces. However, supplies for air units had low priority and aviation gasoline was in critically short supply. Consequently, the day after its arrival in Plaines des Gaiacs, New Caledonia, the 13th Troop Carrier Squadron teamed with two Marine Air Group squadrons and began to haul gasoline and bombs to Henderson Field. It was about 400 miles from New Caledonia to Espíritu Santo, and from Espíritu Santo to Guadalcanal and back to Espíritu Santo was a 1300-mile round trip. Since they were hauling in vitally needed gasoline to Guadalcanal to keep the fighter airplanes flying, they could not refuel there. Also, by having to make the 1,300 miles without refueling, it meant that they could not carry extremely heavy loads on the C-47s.

The route to Guadalcanal was entirely over water and the navigators on the C-47s had to be constantly on their toes, since their only actual navigating experience had been confined to the route overseas—to Hawaii, Christmas, Canton, Fiji, and on to New Caledonia. There were no fighter planes available for escort. The unarmed transports were strictly on their own, and they made a permanent niche for themselves in Aviation's Hall of Fame during those hectic touch-and-go days when American forces were trying so desperately to maintain their toe hold in the South Pacific.

On the night of October 11, 1942, a United States naval force comprised of two heavy and two light cruisers, with destroyer escorts, made a daring midnight interception of some Japanese reinforcement ships, known as the "Tokyo Express." The American vessels tore into the Japanese with their powerful guns and succeeded in sinking three Japanese cruisers, five destroyers, and an auxiliary ship, with the loss of hundreds of men. The American Navy lost one destroyer and 175 men. But the heavy losses did not stop the Japanese. The American cruiser force had to withdraw from the immediate battle area because of a shortage of fuel oil and ammunition for the big guns, and the Japanese immediately resumed operation of their "Tokyo Express." With little to oppose them, the Japanese intensified their naval fire and air attacks on Henderson Field.

Finally, on October 13, all American air operations on Henderson Field had to be canceled because the aviation gasoline was almost exhausted. That night enemy bombers flew across the field and dropped flares to light it brightly. Then Japanese cruisers and battleships standing offshore began pasting the airfield with everything they had. They had no difficulty in directing the fire exactly where they wanted it because of the helpful assistance of the burning flares. The field was shelled most of the night and then enemy bombers took over and blasted it until dawn.

The next morning the American troops looked out across the debris-laden, bomb-pocked airfield and their hopes fell. The Japanese had done an excellent job. They not only had gained the upper hand again in the seesaw battle but it looked this time as if they would hold it if a miracle didn't happen soon. Of the nearly seventy aircraft the Americans had had the day before, there were now only a dozen that could fly because the shelling had knocked out fifty-seven of them. Also, the antiaircraft batteries and the air-warning systems were barely operable.

But the defenders of Guadalcanal were not quitters. Theirs was the only Allied airfield in that area and they were determined to hold it at all costs. They went to work immediately to repair the damaged main strip. Meanwhile, other troops cleared the grass strip which paralleled Henderson

The grandfather of all Gooney Birds is the one and only DC-1 shown here in its TWA markings. It was used as a "flying laboratory" and set many national and international speed records. In February, 1935, TWA loaned it to the National Aeronautic Association to attempt to set new speed, distance and load records. On April 30, 1935, the DC-1 became the first commercial plane in history to span the U.S. continent in less than half a day.

(U.S. Air Force photo)

The test program for X223Y—the Department of Commerce number for the DC-1—was extensive. On one occasion, a mix-up of signals in the cockpit caused an early retraction of the gear on takeoff. The results are shown here.

(Douglas Aircraft Co. photo)

The DC-2, shown here in American Airlines colors, marked the beginning of the end for the slower, less efficient Ford Trimotors and Boeing 247s.

(American Airlines photo)

The profile of the military counterparts of the DC-3 became familiar on warfronts all over the world. Many of them are still flying today as military, commercial or private transports.   (U.S. Air Force photo)

The equipment in the cockpit of this American Airlines DC-3 is primitive by today's standards but represented the finest available in the late 1930s.

(American Airlines photo)

The workers who rolled the 2000th C-47 off the Douglas production line at Santa Monica were given a special privilege. Publicist Joe Messick chalked his name on the fuselage at the beginning of the day shift. By quitting time, hundreds of signatures had been scrawled on every inch of the plane. Although the chalk had to be rubbed off before the U.S. Army Air Force would accept it, many "Rosie Riveters" managed to write their names and addresses inside the wheel wells and hidden compartments. Mechanics in the war zones who found these sent "pen pal" letters from all over the globe. (Douglas Aircraft Co. photo)

Interior of a military C-39, one of the first versions of the Douglas twin-engine transport manufactured for the U.S. Army Air Corps. The radio operator's position shown in the rear of the fuselage was moved to the cockpit area behind the co-pilot in later models.

(U.S. Air Force photo)

In the war zones, the Gooney Bird quickly became known as "the airplane that will always come home." This external view shows the damage sustained by one C-47 when it had a midair collision with another plane.

(Douglas Aircraft Co. photo)

The view from inside the fuselage after the midair collision. This rugged veteran returned safely to its base despite the serious structural damage to its center section. (Douglas Aircraft Co. photo)

The military versions of the DC-3 had small plastic inserts in each of the side windows. The reason is shown here. The unarmed transports, extremely vulnerable to attacking enemy fighters, could use the firepower of the troops on board for protection. Although no enemy aircraft are known to have been shot down in this manner, Army troops felt less like sitting ducks while being transported. (Douglas Aircraft Co.)

The vulnerability of the C-47 to enemy fire from the air and ground was solved by the installation of two .50 caliber machine guns in the aft fuselage. Shown here in action are the "inventors" Colonel Charles D. Farr (left) and Captain John A. McCann, then with the 315th Troop Carrier Squadron.

(Photo from John A. McCann)

A C-47 has just crashed and burned after being shot down by a strafing Japanese fighter at an American air base in China. The dead Chinese coolie had been working on the runway when the enemy plane made its first pass.

(Douglas Aircraft Co. photo)

Their motto was "You Call—We Haul." Here a C-47 of the Troop Carrier Command drops supplies to engineers building an airstrip on Bougainville Island in the Southwest Pacific during World War II.

(Douglas Aircraft Co. photo)

The first C-47 to land on Cyclops Airdrome, Hollandia, New Guinea, taxis past a burned Japanese Zero. (Douglas Aircraft Co. photo)

New Guinea natives crowd curiously around a C-47 which has just landed. C-47s sustained the aerial lifeline between supply bases in Australia and advanced bases to support the "island hopping" strategy of Gen. Douglas MacArthur.
(Douglas Aircraft Co. photo)

A lone C-47 drops food and medicine to American prisoners-of-war on Corregidor. Note the barracks buildings which had been gutted three years before by the Japanese. (Douglas Aircraft Co. photo)

Before the Philippines were liberated, Skytrains of the 317th Troop Carrier Group dropped infantrymen of the 503rd Parachute Battalion on "Old Topside."
(Douglas Aircraft Co. photo)

Fleets of C-47s were used to support the invasion of France during World War II. Hundreds of paratroopers were dropped by parachute and many more came in gliders towed by C-47s. Supplies, medicine and ammunition were dropped to sustain the advance. When airfields were available, C-47s evacuated the wounded.
(Douglas Aircraft Co. photo)

The C-47 could be converted from a cargo to an air evacuation plane in a matter of minutes. Stretchers were stacked four high. Two nurses are shown here tending the wounded while a medical technician assists. The C-47 was used for medical evacuation during World War II, Korea and Vietnam.

(Douglas Aircraft Co. photo)

One of the strangest hybrids of the Gooney series was the DC-2½ shown here. The right wing of a China National Airways Corporation DC-3 had been damaged by Japanese bombs. The only replacement wing available was for a DC-2. It was flown to the spot and fitted into place. Although the pilot reported the DC-2½ had a tendency to roll toward the shorter wing, he had no great difficulty in flying it to its destination.   (Douglas Aircraft Co. photo)

The China National Airways Corporation DC-3 is shown beside the bomb crater after an attack by Japanese bombers. The damaged wing was removed and refitted with the wing from a DC-2. (Douglas Aircraft Co. photo)

Students at the U.S. Navy's parachute rigger's school at the Lakehurst Naval Air Station were required to make jumps with 'chutes they had packed. Here, they are making jumps from an R4D, the Navy's version of the Gooney Bird.
(U.S. Navy photo)

U.S. 503rd Parachute Infantrymen landing in New Guinea during World War II. Several of the parachutes are seen in various stages of opening, swinging the men at precarious angles very close to the ground. (U.S. Air Force photo)

The rate of casualties was considered low as paratroopers jumped from C47s over the Camalaniugan airstrip on the island of Luzon, June, 1945. One trooper was killed and 56 injured. Twenty-three generals made the jump that day.

(U.S. Air Force photo)

Group of U.S. paratroopers seated in C-47 just before takeoff on a mission into France after D-Day. Paratrooper in foreground is holding a bazooka.

(U.S. Air Force photo)

The first plane to land on a permanent airfield in France after D-Day was this C-47 bringing in supplies for the airborne troops that had built the airstrip.

(U.S. Air Force photo)

Waves of American paratroopers drop from Troop Carrier C-47s near Grave, Holland. Livestock graze peacefully near gliders, which had landed earlier with airborne troops. (U.S. Air Force photo)

Parachutes fill the sky over the coast of southern France after the 12th Troop Carrier Air Division's C-47s carried men and supplies to drop zones over the new beachhead. The scene is somewhere between Nice and Marseilles. (U.S. Air Force photo)

C-47s practice snatching gliders at a U.S. base in Texas. The arresting pick-up gear under the belly of the C-47 has just made contact with the nylon rope hooked to the nose of the CG-4A glider. The towrope had been elevated upon the two uprights that may be seen falling away. The system was perfected by All-American Airways (now Allegheny Airlines) for mail pickups prior to World War II.

From a base somewhere in Italy, C-47s of the 51st Troop Carrier Wing line up prior to a mission. They later dropped British paratroopers into Greece and towed gliders loaded with British infantry. They then dropped food and medicines to starving Athenians. (U.S. Air Force photo)

while the Japanese kept up a steady shelling on the workers. Enemy bombers and fighter planes were now free to bomb and strafe without fear of opposition or interception and they struck twice without warning, causing more damage and casualties.

By using the gasoline found in the few drums around the strip and draining fuel from damaged planes, eleven dive bombers managed to stagger into the air late on the afternoon of October 14, but they were a haggard lot and the damage they did to the Japanese was negligible. They sought out the Japanese convoy, determined to send it to the bottom of the sea, but the Japanese shooed them off like so many flies, shooting down two of the attackers with antiaircraft fire.

Now the gasoline was completely gone from Henderson Field and the fighters had succeeded only in making the Japanese more determined than ever. There was enough gasoline left for only one airplane to fly, and to get this, they had to drain the tanks of the remaining flyable airplanes. Late in the afternoon one lone P-40 staggered off under a load of two 500-pound bombs. In a short time the pilot returned and reported that he had scored two hits. It was a pretty good score for one airplane, but a weak attempt at dislodging the enemy.

That night an enemy convoy anchored offshore only ten miles from Henderson Field, between Kokumbona and Tassafaronga. Instead of being a piecemeal reinforcement effort by naval combat craft, these ships were laden with ten thousand Japanese troops and their equipment. While the enemy troop transports unloaded their human cargo, Japanese *Zeros* patrolled the skies above them.

October 15, consequently, seemed like doomsday to the Americans on Guadalcanal; at least it started out that way. But shortly before noon the silhouettes of airplanes were spotted coming from the south and when they came closer the troops could identify them as American C-47s. Strangely, they were not intercepted and one by one the transports came in for a landing. The defenders wasted no time unloading the precious drums of gasoline from each plane. Each load was enough to keep twelve fighters in the air for one hour, and the transports came and went all day— bringing in gasoline and taking out wounded men. The fighter planes at Guadalcanal had teeth again; they could fly and fight back instead of being wiped out helplessly on the ground. The pilots were jubilant. They looked at the slow, lumbering C-47s and felt a great tenderness for the flying boxcars and the pilots who were flying them. These planes had no armor, no guns, no great speed, and little maneuverability. It took a certain kind of guts to fly planes like that into enemy-dominated airspace.

One Navy pilot, looking at the pilots of the C-47s as they helped unload the drums of gasoline, exclaimed, "They couldn't sell me on that run even if they exempted me from paying income tax for the rest of my life. It's the suspense that's so hellish. A fighter pilot always has the feel of a good, fast plane strapped to his rear end with plenty of power at his fingertips. Flying those transports you're just cold turkey for anybody who sets his sights on you. All you can do is stay in the clouds, and if there are no clouds you have no choice but to dive for the ocean and skim the waves all the way home. Do that seven days a week with a few tons of high explosives and inflammables for cargo and you can call yourself a hero in any man's war."

Between the time the transports brought in the first loads of gasoline until they were ready to depart, the flyable fighters had refueled and were ready to take to the air again. Japanese ships were so close to Henderson now that the fighters were over their targets almost as soon as they were airborne. They dived through intense antiaircraft fire to release their bombs. A swarm of enemy *Zeros* arrived and the few American fighters that were flying more than evened the score with the Japanese for that day. The score in three successive attacks was one naval transport exploded and sunk, two damaging hits on other vessels, and one probable.

As far as aerial combat was concerned the score was even—one *Zero* for one American fighter.

Although the damage to the Japanese forces wasn't as great as the Americans would have liked, it was still a great victory for the American airmen. The Japanese had something to fear now that the defending fighter pilots could fight back. If the C-47s could keep the gasoline funneling into Guadalcanal the American pilots had a good chance of nibbling at the Japanese fleet until it would be either sunk or forced to withdraw to safety.

B-17s arrived from Espíritu Santo and joined the fighters in their attack on the Japanese naval vessels. They sank several vessels and routed the Japanese Navy, but the enemy transports left empty—they had, during the night, deposited their human cargo on the Guadalcanal beaches. The bedraggled, tired American ground troops now had to face new and fresh enemy soldiers.

The final outcome is well known, but all that saved these weary troops was the ground support action provided by the American fighter planes. And had it not been for the C-47s which shuttled back and forth from Espíritu Santo to Henderson Field with their loads of precious gasoline, victory would never have been possible.

Official records do not reveal exactly how many C-47s participated in the Guadalcanal action, but it was a combined operation by Army and Marine pilots. The transport pilots and crews soon became hardened to the peppering fire they often received from Japanese small arms and the word "combat" began to take on a new meaning. The defenseless transports were affectionately dubbed "the only unarmed fighters in the world" by their daring pilots. Some of these same transports that helped save Guadalcanal later went on to other islands.

During the New Guinea campaign, the 317th Troop Carrier Group, under the command of Colonel John H. Lackey, had the unglorious job of hauling supplies in to war-weary troops operating against the Japanese in the dense jungle areas. To the troops on the ground there was nothing more pleasing to the eye than an old Gooney Bird circling to deposit bundles by parachute into the small clearings. On almost every mission the C-47s were fired upon by small arms from the ground. Many a transport was peppered by Japanese bullets.

When the 317th moved to the Philippines it was assigned an assortment of missions quite unlike any it had performed in New Guinea. On February 15, 1945, the Battle of Manila was on. The fighting raged in the streets and fierce artillery duels took place as American and Japanese forces fought for control of the city.

On a two-lane dirt highway within sight of the fighting, C-47s of the 317th "Jungle Skippers" landed and took off again on a rigid, preplanned schedule. Crews loaded American wounded onto litters in the C-47s, while less seriously wounded, the walking casualties, climbed into the bucket seats. In the few hours prior to the landing of the transports these men had been wounded on the streets of Manila. Less than an hour away were clean beds, good food, baths—things the men had almost forgotten existed.

The highway airfield was a far cry from most of the landing strips General Kenney's Far East Air Forces had used prior to the Battle of Manila. This highway would have been a tree-lined boulevard if the Japanese had not so rudely interrupted a developer's dream for a Manila suburban real-estate project. As it was, only the roadbed for the ambitious project had been completed, and a fortunate thing it was for the wounded on this particular day. Had the project been completed, there would have been stately trees lining the street, making it impossible to land an airplane.

While all this was happening, the first American C-47s were landing on nearby Clark Field. The Air Force plan had been to use Clark Field as a tactical air base as soon as possible after its capture. But pre-invasion bombing of rail facilities precluded the possibility of immediately using the railroad from Manila, and the roads leading from the beaches of Lingayen Gulf and Subic Bay were too clogged with military traffic to depend on supply by motor convoy. Aviation gasoline, bombs and ammunition had to be flown in quickly in order that Fifth Air Force fighters and bombers could continue, uninterrupted, their relentless campaign against the enemy from the Philippines to China, Indo-China, and Formosa. Service squadrons, combat engineers, signal corps and antiaircraft units, as well as ground personnel and the equipment of fighter and bomber groups, had to be brought in from Leyte and Mindoro Islands. So C-47s were chosen as the means to bring in the necessary men and supplies.

For the next two months the Jungle Skippers streamed in and out of Clark Field to accumulate more than 2,500 planedays of air supply. Filipino crews unloaded bombs, ammunition, and gasoline from the C-47s while other transports circled above waiting for a chance to land with new loads. The airplanes flew with minimum fuel in their tanks so that just a few more bombs or a few more drums of gasoline could be carried on each trip. During these two months the Jungle Skippers hauled more than 3,300 men and over 16 million pounds of cargo to Clark Field. This cargo included nearly 7 million pounds of bombs and almost 3½ million pounds of gasoline.

The many men and women who had served time in the Japanese prison camps on Luzon were glad to see the C-47s. For these hungry, emaciated, disease-ridden Americans who had waited so long, the C-47s meant home, families, freedom.

During the first days of fighting at Manila the C-47s had to land under artillery fire. Sometimes they made their approaches under the trajectory patterns of American artillery. Some areas of the airfield still contained mines, making it extremely hazardous for taxiing airplanes.

When the C-47s had to remain overnight at Clark Field, the air crews guarded their own planes to keep the Japanese from sabotaging them during the night. On at least two

occasions night-marauding Japanese slipped through the
sentry lines and damaged several C-47s with hand grenades.
Occasionally the night guards exchanged shots with shadowy
figures hiding in the tall grass beside the airfield.

The Jungle Skippers were given a new task in April 1945.
Corregidor Island, which had been the last American stronghold in the Philippines, had now to be wrested from the
equally tenacious Japanese. The Skippers were assigned to
haul the 503rd Parachute Infantry Combat Team and drop
them on "Old Topside," as Corregidor was called. First,
however, "Old Topside" had to be softened up.

First, A-20 light attack planes and B-24 heavy bombers
attacked the island. After one wave of aircraft loosed its
fury, another wave took its place, until it seemed that not a
Japanese soldier could possibly be left alive. The Army planners knew this was not true, however. The Japanese were
dug in. It would take men with rifles, bayonets, hand grenades, and flame throwers to completely dislodge them.

Six minutes after the last bombing plane passed over Corregidor, a lone C-47 winged in over the island fortress
carrying heavily armed men of the 503rd Combat Team. The
Jungle Skippers had worked all the way through the islands,
fighting at Nadzab and in other New Guinea campaigns.
The crewmen remembered the Nadzab jump because of the
broad, grass-covered plains on which the paratroopers had
landed. It was difficult to miss such a large expanse of target
area. But Corregidor was different. It was small, barely a
thousand feet square—too small for a three-element drop.
The fortress island was to be the ultimate test of all the experiments that had taken place during the previous two-and-a-
half years in the Southwest Pacific.

"Old Topside" also had other obstacles, which made this
mission the most hazardous ever faced by paratroopers.
Sticking up everywhere were jagged stumps and the ruins of
old buildings. Shell holes completely dotted the island. At
the edge of the 1,000-foot-square the land dropped abruptly
500 feet to the sea on three sides. On the fourth side Correg-

idor narrowed to a small neck, with huge concentrations of Japanese on the other side. The jump would have to be accurate. To miss the plateau would mean to drop into the sea.

The *Skytrains*, as the Gooneys were officially called, came in a long chain, single file, seemingly endless and parachutes blossomed beneath them as paratroopers leaped. Because the jump area was so small, the planes were not able to drop their entire loads on the first pass. Each plane dropped ten men and then went around for a second pass to drop the others. This meant a smaller concentration of men on the ground in the initial jumps to battle the Japanese who were left alive.

The Japanese were in a quandary. Their big guns, captured from the Americans three years before, were trained toward the sea where the U. S. Navy invasion fleet continually harassed them. They had never expected an invasion by paratroopers. The antiaircraft guns on the island had been silenced by the preceding attack planes and bombers. As a result, the *Skytrains* were unmolested. The brilliant orange-and-white parachutes offered a strange contrast to the ruggedness of the island as the men and equipment floated down on the defending Japanese.

While the paratroopers dropped toward the shell-scarred earth, the A-20s returned to pin down the Japanese and to make it easier for the paratroopers to gather their equipment and dig in. The planes roared over the neck of the island with their .50-caliber nose guns biting at the Japanese positions and created an effective curtain of lead for the soldiers.

The fight lasted all morning and the Americans seized their first objectives sooner than they had anticipated. The *Skytrains* appeared again shortly after noon and dropped more paratroopers to deal the final knockout punch to the already groggy Japanese. "Old Topside" was once more in American hands. Airpower, the forerunner in every important move in the Southwest Pacific area, enabled the Americans to have the proudest day of vengeance since the war began. And the first American troops were delivered to Corregidor by the C-47 workhorse of the Army Air Forces.

Corregidor was not the last of the islands in the Philippines to be taken. In other places a few Japanese still held out to the bitter end, sniping whenever they could find a target. Resistance was especially bitter on a tiny land dot in the Manila Harbor entrance called Carabou Island.

American fighters and bombers had clobbered the island until the enemy's heavy weapons were useless, leaving the Japanese with only rifles and pistols with which to protect themselves. Ordinarily the fact that Japanese still held out on this tiny piece of rock would not have been serious, but Liberty ships going into Manila had to pass close to Carabou and the Japanese snipers picked off crew members easily at that range.

Carabou Island, made of solid rock and coral, about 100 yards wide and 600 yards long, was honeycombed with caves which kept the Japanese comparatively safe from bombing and strafing raids. A way had to be found to drive them out.

Since the C-47 was capable of flying at fairly slow speeds, could it be used to spread napalm over the island to burn out the enemy?° Two airplanes and crews of the 317th were selected to try. The planes were loaded with fourteen 55-gallon drums of napalm each and sent on their way. The pilot of the lead plane, Major Archie G. Burdette, described this unique bombing mission:

"I don't know who got the bright idea of going in and burning the Japs out," Burdette said, "but they figured we could spread fire all over the island and drive them out of their holes. When that smoke gets down into the holes, they have to come out. They can't breathe.

"I instructed Captain Sheridan, pilot of the other plane, to circle and observe me as I made my first pass, explaining

___

° Napalm is a jellied gasoline mixture which will ignite upon impact because of a small white phosphorus incendiary bomb attached to it.

that if I ran into serious trouble dropping my load that he was to return to base and not attempt to drop his. All it takes is one well-placed bullet in a can of napalm, and that's all, brother. Napalm's miserable stuff.

"I came in about 50 feet high over the island and slowed the Gooney Bird down to ninety-five miles-per-hour. At that speed and altitude you're a dead duck for a man with a gun if he knows how to use it. I dropped my first barrel of fire on one end of the island. On my reverse pass I dropped another one just as I crossed the near end of the island; then I saw something on the ground that made me wish I hadn't made this second run.

"A Japanese soldier was standing directly in the path of my airplane shooting at us with a pistol. At that distance I didn't see how he could miss. I felt something strike the plane but we passed over him and my 'kicker' released another barrel of fire on the other end of the rock.

"On my next trip around I was determined to get the man who was shooting at us, providing he didn't get a lucky shot into the old Goon first. We dropped a barrel on the end of the island, then another at the Japanese soldier who was still plugging away at us. We missed both targets.

"Next time I figured it was going to be that Jap soldier or me. My sole aim on this run was to drop a barrel right on top of him. I dropped lower, slowed my airplane a little more, and told the kicker what I intended to do. We didn't get our signals crossed either. The next time around there was a mass of fire where the soldier had been standing, but we didn't see the soldier. I knew several bullets had hit my C-47, but I didn't know how many. Sheridan dropped his load of napalm and when we finished the island was a mass of flames and smoke.

"When I got back to the base and landed, I counted nine bullet holes in my Gooney Bird, but there were none in Sheridan's. Funny thing about that ninth hole—the first eight showed where the bullets had entered the fuselage and where they had gone on through, but the ninth one puzzled me until we finally figured out what happened. You see, there was only an exit point for the bullet—no place of entry. Since part of the cargo door had been removed and was open in flight, we concluded that the bullet had entered through the door, probably glanced off one of the napalm drums that were piled in the doorway, and smashed through the side of the airplane. It's a good thing that napalm drum was struck only by a glancing blow. Had it been a direct hit, we would all have been blown sky high.

"Well, we gave a repeat performance of the morning mission, except that we were more selective with our targets the second time. We aimed directly at the caves where the Japs were dug in, and we learned what a good bomber the old C-47 can be when given the chance.

"About the only noteworthy part of the incident is the fact that it was written up by the Public Information Office and circulated widely in newspapers back home. The PIO release claimed that this was the only officially scheduled bombing mission made by a C-47 during the war."

Perhaps this was the only *officially scheduled* C-47 bombing mission of the war, but another World War II pilot might contest the statement because he said he flew the first. . . .

Major Richard L. Benjamin was attached to the First Air Commando Group in India, an outfit commanded by the famous Colonel Philip Cochran (Flip Corkin of comic-strip fame) and Colonel John Alison, which had been flying men and supplies to points beyond the Japanese lines in Burma. The First Air Commando Group had as the backbone of its operation, thirteen C-47s, each of which could tow two gliders. Dick Benjamin was one of these C-47 pilots.

One night in 1944 as he was returning home after delivering a couple of gliders loaded with headache materials for the Japanese, Benjamin saw a string of enemy trucks rolling slowly along a narrow mountain road toward Imphal Valley.

He returned to the base and reported his sighting to his boss.

"Too bad we can't do anything about it," his commander said, shrugging. "Our bombers and fighters are on another big deal tonight. It's a shame to let those trucks get through, but. . . ."

Major Benjamin had already mentally turned his Gooney Bird C-47 into a B-47 and now he sold his boss on the idea. Ground crews quickly shoved three 500-pound bombs and several boxes of fragmentation bombs into the Gooney. Major Benjamin, Lieutenant R. T. Gilmore, Sergeant J. H. Webb, Sergeant R. D. Alexander, and Corporal R. A. Royce piled in and took off. About forty-five minutes later they sighted the convoy.

Since there was no bombsight in the C-47, Benjamin explained to the crew that he would have to estimate the bomb release point. And since there was no bomb release either, the men would have to roll the bombs over the side at his command. However, they had dropped enough bundles to friendly troops in the jungle to make their judgment fairly accurate.

The Japanese trucks moved slowly, the drivers unsuspecting, as Benjamin made a wide reconnaissance sweep around the convoy to fool the Japanese commander.

"We couldn't very well miss," Benjamin said. "It was a narrow canyon and we were only three thousand feet up. Over the target Webb and Royce kicked out the three big bombs, destroying at least one truck. I made another run and the crew peppered the Japanese with the little frag bombs. Even Lieutenant Gilmore went back and joined in. We had a helluva lot of fun for a few minutes.

"When we turned for home we could see several burning trucks, and by the light of the fires we saw Japanese dashing around like ants whose hill had been bashed in by a farmer's boot.

"The Japanese were so surprised to have a C-47 bombing

them that they didn't fire a single shot," Benjamin concluded. "Safest mission I ever flew."

The following night Benjamin and his crew were back to
dragging gliders, but he had proven that many months of
bundle dropping in the jungles could pay off.

In spite of seemingly insurmountable obstacles, Major Ray
Van Diver was a pilot who could be counted on to deliver
the goods at the proper time and place. If he made a mistake, he was quick to rectify it. Flying a C-47 in the South
Pacific to support General MacArthur's "island hopping" campaign, his mission was to fly combat cargo to front-line
troops.

Three American fighter pilots had been forced down near
a small island and had to swim to shore. Van Diver's job
was to locate them and drop emergency rations and survival
gear so they could hold out until a rescue launch or flying
boat could pick them up.

Finding the island, Van Diver circled it. Soon, three
bedraggled figures darted out of the jungle and waved
desperately to the C-47 overhead. Van Diver saw them,
made a low pass to be sure they were Americans.

On his second pass he signaled the crew chief to toss out
the bundle of supplies. The crewman kicked it out and Van
Diver banked the airplane to watch the bundle drop. It
dropped, all right, into six fathoms of water about fifty
yards from shore.

Van Diver was mad, and he knew the men on the beach
were mad, too. He knew that if he were down there and
some stupid, irresponsible pilot missed his target that far,
he'd want to shoot the scoundrel.

As he circled, wondering what to do to rectify the error,
the figures on the beach stood with hands on hips glaring
upward. Van Diver was glad they didn't have a machine
gun.

"I can't leave them there," he muttered. "I wonder if I
could set this bird. . . ."

He banked the airplane steeply. "Gear down!" he yelled to the copilot.

Looking at Van Diver in amazement, the copilot hesitated.

"Gear down, man! Go on—put it down!" Van Diver yelled.

The copilot, still not quite certain what Van Diver had in mind, slowly shoved the gear handle down, waited for the hydraulic pressure to rise, and then locked it.

Van Diver stared intently at the beach rushing up to meet his airplane. "Full flaps!"

The beach was wide enough, but Van Diver was more concerned with the debris scattered across the sand. One half-hidden, well-placed log or rock could cook their goose.

His wheels touched easily, cushioned by the soft sand, and he soon braked to a careful stop. The three airmen ran to the plane, got in, and Van Diver roared off the sand as if it were a paved runway and he did this kind of thing every day. Actually, it was the first time such a landing and takeoff had ever been attempted—with successful results—under these conditions.

After takeoff the flyers went into the cockpit. One said, "Boy, were we glad to see you! If you hadn't landed and picked us up, no telling how long we'd have stayed there."

"Think nothing of it, lads," Van Diver shouted over the noise of his engines. "It was routine. But do me one favor when you get back, will you?"

"Sure," the fighter pilots echoed. "Anything."

"Just don't tell the Old Man I dropped that bundle in the ocean."

On the other side of the world the Gooney Bird played the key role in the initial phases of the first full-scale American airborne operation in history. There was disagreement among intelligence officers regarding the probable attitude of the French forces in Oran. Negotiations on the highest command level to get French co-operation instead of resistance had preceded the proposed invasion of North Africa. In the absence of definite knowledge as to what the French attitude would be on D-Day, two plans had been prepared for the airborne phase, one to be used in case the other proved inappropriate.

One, predicated on French resistance and known as the "War Plan," called for seizing the military airfield at Tafara-oui, seventeen miles from Oran, by an American airborne battalion. The other plan, known as the "Peace Plan," called for the battalion to land at La Senia, a commercial airfield located five miles from Oran. There, it was hoped, they would be welcomed by the friendly population.

On November 7, 1942, the paratroopers stood by their planes in England on five-minute alert. They had been briefed to put the War Plan into action. While they waited, however, the instructions were changed to the Peace Plan. This change confused the troops and the alert was slackened, because the Peace Plan called for a later arrival in Algeria than was called for in the War Plan.

A short time later the action was changed back to the War Plan, but the word did not filter down to the airborne troops and flight crews. Even the mission commander for the airborne forces did not know that the scheme had reverted back to the War Plan!

Paratroopers of the 503rd Parachute Infantry were committed to the operation, and thirty-nine C-47s from the 60th Troop Carrier Group were to take them to Algiers. The airplanes were organized into four flights and were to depart from two air bases—one at St. Eval and the other at Predan-neck, in England. These bases were approximately 1,250 miles from the intended drop zone.

The operation was so involved and so highly classified that even the briefing officers did not know all the details of the nonstop flight. Presumably it was originally intended that the airplanes would fly directly to La Senia only under the Peace Plan. It would have been necessary to refuel at Gibraltar only under the War Plan, so that the airplanes could have fuel enough to return to a friendly base after dropping the troops.

Not only was the briefing inadequate but apparently there was a mistake in the "Signal Annex" of the Operations Order which caused confusion regarding the wavelength of the guide boat stationed in the Mediterranean. Nevertheless, the first flight took off at 9:05 P.M. on November 7, 1942. The flight crews and paratroopers, having stood around waiting for the go signal, were already dog-tired. The flight crews had 1,250 long miles ahead of them—1,250 miles of low-level, long-distance navigation, mostly over water.

The four flights rendezvoused over Portreath, England, and several collisions were narrowly averted while the planes were attempting to assemble in formation in the blackness of night. Finally, in loose formation, they headed south toward Oran.

The flight crews took caffein pills and drank coffee to stay awake. The paratroopers dozed. The airplanes belted in and out of rainstorms; radios, lights, and instruments malfunctioned and caused great anxiety. The crews did everything they could to stay alert, but fatigue took its toll. The formation slowly disintegrated as individual planes climbed to 10,000 feet to clear the mountains of northern Spain. Several planes were fired upon by antiaircraft guns along the northern coast of Spain. At this point three airplanes abandoned the flight. One later landed at Gibraltar and the other two at Casablanca.

By daylight three more planes, low on fuel and with the pilots near exhaustion, landed in Spanish Morocco. For some unknown reason all the paratroopers jumped from one C-47 in Morocco, consequently the troops, flight crews and three airplanes were interned.

Thirty-nine C-47's had started toward Algiers, but when morning came on November 8 only thirty-two, with weary paratroopers and half-dead flight crews, were over the Oran area.

The mission commander, Colonel William C. Bentley, still believed that the Peace Plan was in effect, so he ordered the paratroopers in twelve airplanes to jump after he sighted a

column of tanks near Lourmel. After the troopers jumped,
the tanks were discovered to be American; so the paratroopers
had to be marched toward Tafaraoui.

One of the transports flew low over Tafaraoui and was
shot at by antiaircraft guns, a greeting which did not indicate peace. That C-47 pilot warned the other pilots, then
selected a suitable place to land at the western end of
Sebkra Dioran, a large salt lake south of Oran. He landed
and other planes followed until twenty-eight C-47s were on
the ground there. One of the first planes to land was fired
upon by two Arab horsemen. A bullet detonated a hand
grenade attached to the belt of a paratrooper, killing him
and wounding an airborne officer.

The flight crews dispersed the planes quickly, as the paratroopers—now at about half their original strength—organized
defense posts. But all was quiet and there was no opposition.

The plane carrying Col. Bentley had not joined the others
in the emergency landing near Tafaraoui. He had ordered
his paratroopers out when he sighted the tank column and
then had gone on to reconnoiter La Senia and Tafaraoui. He
saw evidence of ground fighting near the airdrome, and
while his plane circled it was fired upon by antiaircraft
guns.

Suddenly one of the engines spluttered, out of fuel.
Finding a suitable landing area, the pilot quickly landed.
Colonel Bentley got in touch with the American ground
headquarters by radio to discuss the situation, and, while he
was talking, another C-47 landed near by.

It wasn't long before French police appeared from Oran
and took Bentley and the two flight crews into custody. En
route to Oran they were joined by the crew and the paratroop detachment of a third C-47 which had landed in the
same area earlier. They were held for three days in the St.
Philippe Prison Camp before they were liberated.

Meanwhile, on the afternoon of November 8, Lieutenant
Colonel Edson D. Raff, even though injured, organized the
airborne troops to support the attack against Tafaraoui air-

drome. He had apparently received a report that the airfield had been taken and he ordered the C-47s to land there and drop off the rest of the airborne troops. This almost proved fatal, because the C-47s were attacked by both Americans and French as they landed. American pilots flying British *Spitfires* fired on the first transports to land, but did not hit any of them. Several French bombers parked near the runway were damaged. One bomber, loaded with bombs, caught fire and exploded. From the surrounding hills French 75s began shelling the runway, and firing continued for an hour. A few C-47s were damaged by shell fragments. Confused air action went on for most of the afternoon, while the Americans slowly mopped up the airfield perimeter and secured the airfield.

Not all the C-47s from the emergency landing area got to Tafaraoui. French fighter planes suddenly attacked the rear-echelon planes. One C-47 was forced down as the pilot attempted to take off and his plane was riddled with bullets. Several paratroopers and crewmen were wounded, four were killed. A copilot was killed while landing and another airplane completely wrecked. A third plane was badly shot up and another became lost and was forced to land at Arzem.

Of the thirty-nine C-47s that had left England on November 7, nine were missing and three were destroyed by the evening of November 8. Of those that reached Tafaraoui, only fourteen were flyable.

On the morning of November 9, the French began shelling the field again. One of the flyable C-47s was damaged and the radio operator wounded. No planes took off that day, but by noon of the following day the French Air Force in Algeria had been neutralized.

On November 11, thirteen C-47s delivered 134 paratroopers to Maison Blanche, and on the same day the first elements of the 60th Troop Carrier ground echelon arrived at Algiers by boat. They were sorely needed.

Although it cannot be said that the first airborne operation was a success, a lot was learned from the snafus that

had developed. It demonstrated the capabilities of the C-47
in long-range operations, in addition to pointing out what
happens when plans are not co-ordinated all the way down
the line. History bares the errors, but it also gives the
figures and statistics necessary for future planners to evalu-
ate the mistakes and prevent them from being made again.

When the air war over Germany raged full scale, and the
huge daylight raids had begun, many a crippled bomber was
escorted by a fighter plane to neutral Sweden, where the
crew was interned. The American and Allied airmen who
found safe refuge in Sweden had to be taken out of the
country and returned to their respective units so they could
fly and fight again. How could it be done? Flying from
Sweden to England meant crossing over or near enemy territory, and German fighter planes patrolled the escape routes,
alert to any attempt by the Allies to rescue their flight crews.

Brigadier General Earl S. Hoag, Commander of the European Division of the Air Transport Command, came up with
the answer to evacuating literally thousands of internees by
taking them across enemy territory on an unscheduled airline
basis.

General Hoag's C-47s, his secret-airline planes, flew only in
bad weather. When the weather was at its worst, the Gooney Birds would sneak across German-held territory, flying
on instruments, land in Sweden and pick up a load of internees. If the weather remained foul, Hoag's crews would
leave Sweden immediately in order to take advantage of the
excellent cloud protection. If, while they were on the
ground, the weather took a turn for the better, the pilots
would wait for bad weather to set in again. Since Sweden
was neutral, there was no fear of *Luftwaffe* attacks even
though the Germans knew all about the operation. The only
things the Germans didn't know about the operation were its
schedule . . . and how to stop it.

Just prior to the invasion of France, Hoag's airline carried
out the entire Norwegian Government-in-Exile and flew them

to London. It hauled out thousands of Norwegian soldiers who had regrouped in Sweden, diplomats and other high officials. Before the invasion of France, 2,000 highly trained Norwegian soldiers were flown across German-occupied Norway to Great Britain despite 250 alerted *Luftwaffe* night fighters, antiaircraft and German coastal guns.

During internment in Sweden, the American crewmen were constantly followed by German Gestapo agents who hoped an American would reveal the airline schedule. They never received a clue. Crewmen's quarters were ransacked by Gestapo agents who looked for any evidence that might divulge the schedule, but they never seemed to understand that there was no schedule and that the airplanes flew only in the worst weather.

Try as they might, the Germans never stopped Hoag's secret airline. They resorted to every trick in the books, but to no avail. The operation continued until most of the internees were removed from Sweden, and, in spite of the bad weather and German efforts to stop them, Hoag lost only one airplane.

Flying in extremely bad weather is nerve-wracking when it is done constantly, but there are occasions when a pilot would welcome a bit of bad weather in preference to a battery of antiaircraft guns lined up on his C-47. Lieutenant Arthur Douglas, a Troop Carrier pilot, almost didn't make it home one night shortly after D-Day. He said later that he had, on that particular night, lived a couple of lifetimes.

Douglas tells his own vivid story:

"From the moment we were briefed and told that this was the real thing, I think all of us wondered how much there was to the old Troop Carrier joke that you train two years for a five-hour job. We were finally going to learn the answer.

"The paratroopers were something to see as they waited for the order to climb into the planes. Some of them seemed very talkative, others relaxed and were at ease, just the way they seemed on practice missions. A few of them spent the last few minutes sharpening a variety of homemade weapons such as spiked brass knuckles and machetes.

"Looking back now, I can say that the takeoff was routine, one airplane and glider lifting from the runway every thirty seconds. But it sure didn't seem routine at the time.

"This was the mission for which we had spent hours and hours of training, and had gone through scores of practice missions both in England and in the States. This one had to be right. If it wasn't, it wouldn't be a case of the Old Man bawling us out. It would mean a messed-up mission. It might slow up the invasion plan, or the paratroopers might be dropped where they could do no good and would be easy prey for the Germans.

"I was flying in the third group to go into our target area. That's a pretty good spot. I was impressed with how peaceful and quiet it seemed as we flew over Britain and crossed the Channel. It didn't seem possible that anything could happen on such a quiet night. We kept good formation all the way over, and I suppose every pilot was probably thinking this would be a milk run.

"Just before I gave the four-minute warning to jump—we would flick the switch which flashed a green light in the fuselage of the plane which meant to paratroopers 'Stand up and hook up'—we ran into the awfullest mess you've ever seen. The whole sky lit up. Jerry started throwing lead as if he owned the ground he was protecting. Red tracers arched up lazily at us and you could see the flashes of the guns on the ground.

"Jerry had our number, all right, because we got hit in the center section. I knew we'd been hit, but I didn't know how serious it was. We kept on flying and I reckoned we hadn't been hurt much. We were about seven hundred feet high at the time, our formation was good, and even though we could see other planes get hit, it looked as if we were going to do all right.

"I flicked the toggle switch for the drop light as we went

over the drop zone and then wheeled for home. Jerry was still throwing up lead and generally making a heel of himself. Naturally we all dived for the deck after we'd dropped our paratroopers. I dropped down to a hundred feet and poured on the coal.

"We were clear out over the coast when my crew chief came up to the cockpit. I said to him, 'How'd it go?'

" 'You still got a plane full of men, Lieutenant,' " the crew chief explained. 'Why didn't you give them the green light?'

"As far as I was concerned, I *had* given them the green light, and I told the crew chief so. He said he'd been back there and the green light didn't show. I had him go back and watch while I tried the light again. It didn't flash, and I knew then that the flak that had hit us had knocked out part of our electrical system.

"There we were over the Channel on our way home. We'd been over the drop zone but hadn't dropped. I wouldn't be able to explain it when I got back, so I had to make up my mind what to do. I sort of figured I had to get those guys back to a place where they could work.

"I don't know why, but I turned back. It felt awfully lonesome going back in one C-47. It wasn't hard to find the way back, but it felt funny flying all by myself. All the Jerry fire would be concentrated on us, and that's exactly what happened. If the first sweep over the drop zone had been warm, the second was hotter than the depot stove.

"As we approached the drop zone, I yelled back 'Get ready to jump!' And at the instant we were over, I yelled 'Jump!' The first man was bracing himself in the door ready to pop out. Believe it or not, at that instant he was hit in the stomach around which he had explosives wrapped—maybe hand grenades. He staggered, looked as if he might clog the door, so the next man gave him a big push out. It was a good thing for all of us that he did, for right then the explosives around his middle went off and the plane jumped and rocked like it had been shot in the tail with rock salt.

"For a minute I was certain we'd had it. When the plane

finally responded to the controls, I held it on course until the paratroopers had time to drop, then I went down to the deck again and started for home.

"By this time I felt sure I had been kicked in the head by a lucky horseshoe. And when the crew chief came up to say that the explosion had knocked down all the men in their heavy equipment and they hadn't been able to regain their feet until we'd passed the drop zone, I felt like the guy who had hit the jackpot twice and wasn't due again for another century or two.

"On the second pass over the drop zone our instruments had been knocked out. I had only my compass and air-speed indicator and the instruments for the right engine. Should I go back a third time or head for home base?

"I'm telling you, that's the time I wished I were back instructing in a school in the States or that I'd gone with the Air Transport Command. There you were, sitting like a crippled duck, nothing to fire back at Jerry with and not even self-sealing gasoline tanks or armor.

"Before I knew it I was making another hundred and eighty degree turn and heading back for the drop zone. Even though I didn't have any instruments, it was easy to find the drop zone by the gunfire—that's where it was the thickest. This time I yelled to get ready before we got to the drop zone, and when we were over it I yelled, 'Get going!'

"This time Jerry had everything out and was shooting at us as if the war depended on his knocking down just us. So we all held our breath, I suppose, and after I had waited long enough for all the men to have jumped I stuck my nose down toward the deck. When I leveled off about a hundred feet above the ground I said to myself, 'I wonder if we're going to have to go back again.'

"When we reached the coast, I turned to see what the crew chief would have to say. The chief said three of the troopers had been knocked out by the bouncing of the plane, and were still aboard. 'Tell them they're going to have to jump tomorrow, because if this crate holds together we're going home right now,' I said to the crew chief.

"The trip back was in the same kind of weather we went out in, and somehow it seemed even more quiet and peaceful. The three paratroopers were not seriously hurt and were sore as the devil because they didn't get out of the plane over the drop zone. I didn't feel up to explaining to them just then that we'd stooged all over Northern France and had already used up all the luck of a couple of lifetimes.

"Although the plane was flying fairly good, I was losing oil pressure. My tanks had been hit. That wasn't good. We lost most of our oil on the way back, and when we got over the airfield I found that my landing gear on the left side had been all shot up. We finally got both wheels down, though, and landed safely. The airplane looked like a sieve but flew again after only a couple of days in the maintenance shed. Believe me, no other airplane on earth could take what that old bird took that day. There never was and never will be another plane like it!"

On March 28, 1944, five C-47s plowed into the darkness to make a pinpoint delivery of supplies on a target in Yugoslavia. The pilots and their crews were tense, because this was the first of a series of missions for the Yugoslav partisans, who were making a last-ditch stand for their country.

Having assigned liaison officers with the partisan groups, the Army Air Forces' 60th Troop Carrier Group worked up a series of signals so the air crews could make certain they were dropping to the partisans and not to the Germans. On the ground the partisans would mark the target area with a triangle, cross or other symbol, and the pilot of the C-47 would flash the "letter of the night." For further identification, the men on the ground would flash back another prearranged letter of the Morse code.

Since the partisans were dug into the hills, practically all the supply drops had to be made in extremely treacherous country. It was usually necessary, therefore, for the planes to fly over the target area several times in order to get all the load out due to the small drop area and the short time they could remain over the target.

After the first series of drop missions, a number of small landing strips were hacked out in partisan territory on which the C-47s could land. More supplies were brought in and personnel evacuated. In a record two-night period fourteen C-47s evacuated 585 children and wounded partisans, an average of 42 people per airplane.

But it wasn't easy to conceal the operation from the Germans, and the partisans were constantly harassed by German commando groups. The partisans, realizing that the American C-47s were the life line to freedom and liberation, mined the roads and paths with explosives and ambushed the Germans with rifles, grenades and homemade weapons.

On one occasion the Germans attacked a landing strip near Tito's headquarters just two hours after six C-47s had taken off. The partisans fought stubbornly for two days against German paratroopers, glider troops, dive bombers, and tanks, finally losing the battle and retreating to the mountains, where they continued the fight for two weeks before the Germans finally pulled out.

Captain John Bowman got the scare of his life one night when a German fighter plane attacked as he was making a landing at an isolated field between two steep mountains. Zigzagging the plane on his final approach, he managed to evade the German's fire. Bowman landed and, followed by his crew, leaped into a nearby foxhole with the partisans. The German didn't press the attack on the ground and the captain realized that the pilot was afraid to make a second pass into the narrow valley. Instead, the German pilot circled high overhead, knowing it would soon be dawn and that the C-47 would be an easy target in daylight.

Bowman couldn't wait for dawn. As soon as his plane was unloaded he took off into the darkness without lights. Risking his life, Bowman flew low until he reached the coast. Flying high above, the German had failed to spot him as he escaped in the lumbering transport.

Sometimes, when landing in the darkness on the short strips, pilots damaged their airplanes by ramming into unseen objects. When this happened, they had to camouflage the planes and remain at the airstrip until the damage was repaired. This often proved risky, especially at night when they had to use lights to work by. That was exactly what the German pilots wanted—they could swoop down and strafe the airplane and mechanics.

Captain Collifer, who flew one of the first missions for the partisans, related one of his experiences:

"It should have been an ordinary short-field landing, but a heavy ground fog caused me to overshoot. We ran off the end of the runway and nosed up, causing slight damage to the props. They stuck firmly in the mud, and there was nothing we could do that night.

"The next day my crew, helped by several stranded bomber crewmen, some partisans, and twenty oxen, pulled the plane out of the mud and we repaired it. All that time we prayed that a German fighter pilot wouldn't spot us, and that day not a single fighter appeared to see what was happening at that airstrip.

"Before we took off that night, the partisans fed us the best they had. It consisted mostly of hot goat's milk, and each of us had eight bowls."

Captain Collifer then took off with his crew and thirty-one stranded bomber members.

Captain Robert Snyder wasn't so fortunate, however. Approaching a drop zone in a small, deep valley, Snyder signaled the partisans that he would make the drop from low altitude so it would be more accurate. He circled the area once, dropped low, and started into the valley. A jagged cliff loomed in front of him and Snyder turned sharply to miss it. The airplane stalled and, at the low altitude, would not respond to the frantic efforts of the pilot to control it. The C-47 crashed, and Snyder and his five crewmen were killed instantly. The partisans buried them with full military honors.

Another pilot, a Lieutenant Houser, came in over a landing strip early one morning and saw a yellow flare on the ground, which meant that the airfield was under attack.

Suddenly a German fighter plane dived on him and sent a 20-mm. shell crashing through his left wing and engine. The airplane caught fire and Houser gave the signal to bail out, as he fought to keep the plane under control. His copilot, Lieutenant Largent, ran to the rear bellowing for the crew to bail out but the airplane lurched, throwing Largent off balance. By the time he regained his senses, the smoke and fire filled the cabin of the C-47 and Largent couldn't tell whether or not the others had bailed out.

Seeing a large hole in the fuselage, Largent groped toward it, fell through, grasped his ripcord and tugged. The chute opened and he was safe. One glance told him, however, that the others had not bailed out. Helplessly, he watched the airplane swerve out of control and crash into the rocky hillside with the other crew members aboard.

For his heroic action in attempting to save the crew and airplane, Lieutenant Houser was awarded the Silver Star posthumously. The following night Largent was flying another mission into partisan territory.

One of the most interesting missions was flown by Lieutenant Harold E. Donohue, who landed on an airstrip less than 600 yards long. One end of the airfield ran straight into the side of a mountain, which meant that he would have to take off in the opposite direction from which he had landed. Normally this would not have caused much anxiety; however, this mission was to evacuate sixty-nine pathetic, scared little children whose ages ranged from six weeks to fifteen years.

Donohue looked at the children, scratched his head and wondered how many he could carry out in one load. Placing them exactly right, filling every bare corner, he crowded all sixty-nine, plus his crew into the plane. Then he wondered whether or not the C-47 would leave the ground with the tremendous load—seventy-four people.

In spite of the rough, short runway, Donohue's Gooney Bird clawed its way into the night, the engines not missing a beat.

Later a crew member said of Donohue, "He's a young fellow, but he's got a kid of his own." That made a difference.

One of the unsung heroes of World War II was the "food kicker," the man who dragged heavy bundles of supplies to the open door of a C-47, took a firm grip on anything solid his hands could reach, and kicked with all his might to push the heavy parcels out to troops eagerly awaiting the supplies on the ground. It wasn't an easy job for several reasons, one of them being that sometimes the "kicker" would lose his grip and follow the bundle down. More often than not, the "kicker" didn't wear a parachute because its bulkiness hampered his movements inside the airplane. Also, many "kickers" were wounded by enemy ground fire as they stood in the open doorway preparing to shove the cargo out.

Accuracy was also a problem and thousands of pounds of precious supplies were lost forever when they missed a tiny clearing and were swallowed up by the jungle. Too many runs were required, causing flight crews to be exposed to enemy ground fire for extended periods.

Research experts at Wright Field, Ohio, considered the problem and finally commissioned the Douglas factory at Oklahoma City to experiment with an airplane employing a double conveyor and with an extra door cut in the fuselage opposite the cargo door.

The first trial run was made over Tinker Field in July 1944. The conveyor dropped its simulated cargo packs within a 400-foot circle in six seconds. Authorities at Wright Field accepted the twin conveyor plane for further exhaustive tests and ordered similar modified equipment to be installed in several C-47s for experimental use in various combat theaters.

A single conveyor with an improved roller launch and a faster belt of greater capacity proved advisable. With the extra door eliminated, the equipment could be installed or removed in an hour at any field base, and the supply-dropping C-47 was not limited to single-purpose usefulness.

Occupying the left half of the C-47 cabin from aft of the pilot's compartment to the cargo door, a distance of 22 feet, the assembly would support about 4,000 pounds on its 22-inch-wide endless belt. Aluminum alloy rollers, mounted one foot apart, supported the ¼-inch impregnated fabric belt with its load.

A 3.87-horsepower electric motor, deriving power from the plane's 24-volt system, drove the belt at approximately six feet per second, clearing its load of parachute-rigged containers in four seconds. The containers, another development of Air Technical Service Command engineers, could be loaded two or three high.

The packs scooted onto a launching platform at the cargo door—a series of tapered roller bearings. Static lines automatically opened the chutes as a guardrail reflector nudged the packages out the door.

Before this new idea in "food kicking" was developed, "food kickers" from Papua to Bastogne had needed a strong back and plenty of leg power to dispatch war stuff to where it would do the most good. But, even by flying the C-47s back and forth at barely more than stalling speed, and only 150 feet or less above hostile ground, the crews could drop only six hundred pounds of cargo at any one time by the old method.

The "kicker" lay on his back, braced himself and, at a given signal from the pilot, the "kicker" kicked and the "pusher" pushed. It took pass after pass to discharge the cargo and at 110 miles per hour the plane was a "sitting duck" for enemy guns. Surprise helped achieve the first pass, but each succeeding pass cut down the percentage of chances for survival. There were instances, too, when a sudden lurch of the plane was the cause of a man being thrown out.

Occasionally the last box, disgorged as the C-47 pulled up for the getaway, struck and damaged the plane's tail. To combat this hazard, Brigadier General Paul H. Prentiss, commanding the Troop Carrier command of the Fifth Air Force, asked Harry Booth, Douglas service engineer in the South

Pacific, to devise a cargo hatch to be cut in the floor of several C-47 "biscuit bombers."

This on-a-dime dropping contrivance was given one of its first combat trials supplying fuel for General Patton's Third Army tanks and trucks while they were outrunning their supplies across France in August of 1944. During these tests clusters of five to seven 5-gallon cans of gasoline were dropped by parachute.

The conveyor device did this much better, however. In one typical sortie the load included 5,000 K rations. Another plane dropped 3,000 pounds of gasoline, almost 500 gallons, in seven seconds and in a space of 300 yards. Thirty-three hundred pounds of water, about 400 gallons, formed part of another load. Hundreds of units of plasma and whole blood were also dropped.

The new invention might have left a few of the "kickers" out of a job after the new mechanical gadget was put to extensive use, but it is doubtful that there were many complaints from the men who had stood in the doorways, inviting the sniper's bullets or waiting to be thrown out by a sudden lurch of the airplane. No one envied the "kicker," nor did anyone ever try to steal his job.

Japanese infantrymen, accustomed to shooting at stationary objects on the ground, tried desperately but vainly to bring down the low-flying Gooneys that resupplied their American enemies. They aimed at the cockpit but, because of the 110-m.p.h. speed of the slow-flying planes when on their drop passes, managed mostly to kill or wound the "kickers" in the rear. The CO of the 443rd Troop Carrier Group, the main supporting airlift unit for British Brigadier General Orde Wingate's Chindit penetration into Japanese-held Burma, came up with an answer. His name was Colonel Charles D. Farr, a former Navy enlisted pilot who "went Air Force" in 1940. Colonel (then Captain) John A. McCann, who was his executive officer, told how he proposed to cut down on the losses of his crewmen:

"Colonel Farr believed that if a 'gun' ship or ships were

fed into these drop patterns, particularly in those areas where high volume of delivery was being affected and where we usually drew a volume of fire, that a good spray job from caliber 50s would suppress hostile ground action against the aircraft.

" 'Mac,' Colonel Farr said to me one rainy night in April 1944 as we sat on the creaky wicker chairs in our basha, nestled between two large revetments at Sylhet, India, 'You're an aerial gunner—why can't we put caliber 50s on a C-47?'

"I'd known Charley only a short time, but well enough to appreciate that he had a real 'hen on' and he wanted to bat the idea around, even though he likely already had it well conceived in his own mind. So I asked, 'Where—in the nose?'

" 'Nope—too much stuff to fool with out there,' he said. He thought some more and then said, "If we made a rig, could you shoot it out of the side window?'

" 'Mebbe,' I replied, 'but you wouldn't get much area of fire and it would take up a lot of valuable room right in the middle of the cargo compartment.'

"Then he said, 'You're probably right—how about out the door? That's it,' he continued. 'Sure, we can rig up a tripod and cut a hole in the aft part of the cargo door.'

" 'You mean mount a flexible fifty and fire it out the door without any safety stops! Charley, the pilots would never sit still for that.'

" 'Oh, yes, they would,' he answered, 'Besides let's not cross that bridge yet.'

"We 'chalk talked' the details with pencil and paper until the colonel had a workable sketch drawn up which he turned over to the maintenance gang the next day. The project was launched.

"C-47 No. 315054 was the first ship cut from the herd to undergo the surgery that would transform this placid beast of burden into a deadly bird of prey. As originally conceived, a large aperture was cut out of the aft half of the double width cargo door from about waist high to slightly above eye level. A tripod of heavy angle iron was attachable by set screws to the floor and lower edge of the new aperture in the aircraft to provide a stable platform for a slotted frame into which neatly fitted the stem of the swivel pin mount of the gun. Thus the gunner standing securely inside the airplane with the gun barrel outside had a radius of action of approximately 160 degrees of transverse, about 80 degrees of elevation and a like amount of declination, minus, of course, the contour of the tail assembly and the wing, about which there still was a lot of pilot head shaking."

The experiments by Farr and McCann were entirely successful and another Gooney was modified the same as the first C-47. Both were used in subsequent drop missions, but no further planes were modified. "The Ugly Duckling of Air Power" as McCann referred to the Gooney, had proved once again that it could do anything—even defend itself if it had to.

The expandable airplane

5

A C-47 is the most air-kindly and forgiving of all air-planes, but you must not abuse it.

—ERNEST K. GANN
Fate Is the Hunter

ACCORDING TO Douglas engineers, the C-47 has a weight limit. In war days, however, pilots paid little attention to limits because of the emergency conditions under which they flew. In one theater the gross weight might be pegged at 28,500 pounds, in another 33,000. One outfit in the Pacific limited the payload to 5,000 pounds of freight because of the need for extra gas tanks, while others said simply, "Cram it in until she won't hold any more."

Although various units had different weight limitations, many of the weights were estimated, because of the lack of scales. There was a job to be done and the loaders did the best they could to load the planes for safe flying.

Some of the first pilots to test the load-carrying capabilities of the DC twin-engine plane were the pilots of the
China National Airways Corporation. A man who was responsible for much of the exploratory flying over the "Hump," and
who set an early passenger-carrying record in a DC-3, was a
CNAC pilot named Moon Chin.

Flying over the rugged China terrain was routine for Captain Chin and he took off from the Chungking airfield with
a load of passengers bound for Myitkyina, a military base in
Burma. Not long after the plane was airborne, a string of
Japanese fighters buzzed in, bent on clobbering the unarmed
transport. Coming in by twos and threes, the fighters
viciously attacked the Douglas. Chin used all the evasive tactics in his book; then dropped down low and flew his transport in and out of the treacherous mountain valleys, finally
landing at a small hidden airstrip to wait for his pursuers to
give up the chase. This was an old game with him.

One of Chin's passengers on the flight was an unshaven,
balding, bedraggled American. He was dressed in a combination of civilian clothing and Army uniform, and Moon
Chin wondered what he was doing on this flight.

On the ground, the American suggested that Chin change
his destination because he had heard that Myitkyina was
now in Japanese hands. Why not go to a field in India that
he was certain was open?

But Chin had been ordered to fly to Myitkyina to evacuate
the airline workers and valuable equipment before the Japanese captured the place. He had not heard that the Japanese
were already there, and for those people Chin's plane, plus
some other CNAC DC-2s and 3s, was the only hope for survival. No, he was sorry but he could not change his destination.

When the plane arrived at Myitkyina the airfield buildings
were in flames and hundreds of people were milling excitedly
around the airdrome. The Japanese fighters had practically
destroyed the airfield, and Chin knew they would soon be
back to finish the job.

At the parking ramp people tried to crowd into the air-

plane with their meager possessions. Many offered Chin
large sums of money, which he refused. At first he permit-
ted thirty desperate souls on board. As others begged tear-
fully, he chose ten more. This seemed as many as he ought
to haul. But there was still space inside, and he squeezed in
ten more, then another ten until sixty people were aboard!

It wasn't an easy take-off on the soft turf, and Chin knew
that the trees on the other end of the field spelled disaster if
the engines missed a beat. The plane was soon airborne,
however, and several hours later he set down at Calcutta.

When the door was opened and the passengers streamed
out, sixty-eight pathetic creatures clumped down the steps to
the firm earth of India. Sixty-eight passengers and a crew of
four made seventy-two on the flight! While he had been
counting the people aboard at Myitkyina, eight stowaways
had hidden in the aft compartment! The tattered American approached Captain Chin as he stared incredulously and
thanked him for the ride. "Believe me, Chin," he began, "if
I had had any idea that you were going to jam that many
people into this old crate I would have gone home the way
I came."

Chin smiled a tired smile. "I'm sorry I alarmed you, my
friend. But, tell me, where did you come from? How did you
get to China?"

This time the American smiled. "I flew in," he said nonchalantly, "by way of Tokyo."

Moon Chin looped his arm around the American. His
passenger was none other than Brigadier General Jimmy
Doolittle returning from his historic B-25 raid on the Japanese capital.

Captain John Mowat had landed his C-47, thinking he had
just flown his last mission before returning to the States from
a long tour in the China-Burma-India Theater. He was jubilant as he watched the ambulance taking away to the Lido
Hospital the load of wounded men he had just flown in. He
had done his share in helping the men who were fighting a

nasty, dirty war, but he was glad the weary routine was finally finished for him.

As Mowat walked away from the Operations shack for what he thought was the last time, the squadron Operations officer called to him, "Hey, John. I got another mission for you."

"Not for me, friend," Mowat said dryly. "I'm going home. So long."

"Not quite, old buddy," the officer said. "The Old Man scheduled this one himself, and you're *it*."

"That do make it different," Mowat growled. "So what's it this time?"

"Ask the boss. He dreamed it up."

Mowat asked the boss, and was told that he was to haul eighty live sheep and drop them to British jungle troops fighting in Burma, so they could have Christmas dinner in style.

"Ugh!" said Mowat. "Mutton? For Christmas dinner?"

That night eighty sheep were jammed into Mowat's airplane. Had there been eighty live sheep and nothing else, John Mowat would have thought nothing of it, but they were only part of his load.

In addition, sixteen Indian sheepherders, each with nearly 200 pounds of baggage, were crammed aboard. All this, plus a crew of three for the Gooney Bird, added up. Nineteen people—roughly 3,800 pounds. Eighty live sheep at about 50 pounds each—4,000 pounds. Mowat could thus count 7,800 pounds without counting the approximately 3,200 pounds of baggage and miscellaneous equipment. Mowat figured he had about 11,000 pounds payload aboard, yet the cargo handlers insisted he had only 9,400 pounds.

John Mowat had flown many heavy loads in this plane, but not one like this flying barnyard. And, as if the extreme load weren't enough, he had to take off at night on an unlighted runway with tall trees towering at the opposite end.

Mowat could tell that this was no ordinary load as he taxied out. This time his plane was stuffed. The wheels ground against the turf and the fuselage squeaked and sagged under the load. He checked the engines—okay. If they weren't he'd know in a few seconds.

The tower cleared him for take-off. He released the brakes and the plane began to move, slowly at first like a Mack truck. About a thousand feet down the runway Mowat forced the tail up; in another thousand feet he had reached an air speed of 60 miles per hour, not enough for take-off. The end of the runway was near. Mowat yelled to his copilot to drop a quarter wing flaps, but this didn't help either, and there was only one thing left to do: haul the plane into the air whether she wanted to leave or not.

Mowat yelled to his copilot, "Hold the throttles forward to the stops!"

Grabbing the control wheel with both hands, he pulled back hard. The plane shook, finally responded to the pressure, and reluctantly left the ground. Not quite ready to fly, the groaning plane bounced down again, only to be yanked back into the air by the stubborn Mowat. The second time in the air it started to mush. Staggering like a drunk, the airplane slowly picked up air speed, then Mowat heard what he hoped he wouldn't—trees scraping the bottom of the fuselage. He eased back ever so slightly on the wheel so he wouldn't stall. He waited for the crash of the limbs, but none came.

Finally getting its wind, the Gooney Bird inched its way into the night sky, and Mowat completed his mission a few hours later. He had set a record of sorts but he would just as soon have left the honor to someone else. The fighting men on the ground had their Christmas dinner and Mowat had at last flown his final mission.

The walk-on type of cargo was not always to be eaten, however. Sometimes the live cargo consisted of mules to be used in their traditional role as beasts of burden by troops on the ground. But how could they be gotten into the dense, treacherous mountains safely?

Someone looked at the old C-47, measured the girth of an average mule and the inside of the plane and conceived the Jackass Airlift.

The Chinese 14th and 22nd Divisions were being sent to Chanyi, China, in December of 1944, because it was believed the Japanese were planning a big push on the city of Kweiyang. The divisions needed ground transportation—horses and mules. These pack animals were in short supply, however, because Mongolia, which had formerly been one of China's principal sources of animals, was now cut off by the Japanese. Tibet was another source, but she could supply China with only about 10,000 horses per year at maximum, many less than the number needed.

The Chinese were not stock raisers and they knew little about the care and breeding of mules and horses. Although they had once attempted breeding by scientific methods, nothing had come of it. Also, battle losses of overworked mules and horses in China had seriously decimated the supply.

The commanders of the two divisions had originally planned to use about 2,500 horses and mules to haul the divisional supplies across the mountains, but further planning indicated that 1,500 might do the job. The problem was how to transport them to China so they would be fresh and capable when they reached the mountains near Chanyi.

The obvious method of transportation was by airplane. The C-47 could do it if stalls were made inside the fuselage to hold the animals in place during flight. Staff Sergeant C. L. Hathaway, from the Corps of Engineers, was assigned the task of rigging the airplanes to carry the animals. The sergeant and his crew of twenty Chinese soldiers had only one day to get an airplane ready for the first flight across the mountains. They began work on December 9, 1944.

First, Hathaway removed the seats from the passenger compartment. His next problem was to build simple but rigid stalls for the animals. He sent his Chinese soldiers scurrying for large bamboo poles.

When they returned with the poles, Hathaway measured the length of the inside of the fuselage. He cut six poles long enough to extend from the cabin door to the rear cargo door, and eight poles the width of the fuselage. Several shorter poles were cut for uprights and lashed against the longer poles. When the poles were cut, fitted together and lashed, there were four separate stalls, with room in each to accommodate an animal and its handler to care for the animal in flight.

This finished, Hathaway knew that he had another problem. During the flight the animals would have to urinate, unless he could persuade them to do so prior to take-off. If they urinated in the airplane it would drain through the floor and corrode the control cables stretching underneath. Hathaway solved the problem by placing a tarpaulin on the floor covered with a piece of coco matting, and spreading 200 pounds of hay throughout the fuselage.

Next came the problem of loading the animals. Hathaway and his men tried using ramps and walking the animals into the cargo door, but for reasons known only to the animals, this failed and they balked at the door. Hathaway finally accomplished the loading by first putting the animals into the rear of a covered truck, then backing the truck up to the cargo door and enticing them inside. Even so, the sergeant and his crew often had to use the push-pull method.

Once inside, the animals were lashed into their stalls by halters which kept their heads held tightly so they could not move freely and injure themselves. In addition, a rope was tied to the side of the fuselage, passed across the backs of the animals and lashed to the other side. The pack saddles were placed on each animal so the ropes would not cut into the flesh should the airplane encounter rough weather.

The "Jackass pilots" took off and climbed to 14,000 feet for the long flight across the Hump into China. Over the Hump the animals were unusually well-behaved, probably because the lack of oxygen took some of the fire out of them, but whenever the C-47s hit rough air the animals pawed and

pranced and became extremely nervous. On one occasion an
animal broke loose inside the airplane. On this particular
flight an aerial engineer was aboard who had been a veteri-
narian in civilian life. He finally persuaded the animal to lie
down in the stall, then sat on its neck until the C-47 landed
at Chanyi.

While several transport units in the CBI *carried* mules, the
315th Troop Carrier Squadron was the only unit to drop
them by parachute. To the uninitiated this may not seem
like a major logistics problem, but to the crews of the 315th
it was.

Imagine for a moment that you are the pilot of a C-47
and your squadron commander orders you to fly a "drop
mission." All you usually need to know is where to drop
whatever you are going to drop and when you are expected
to drop it. But today your CO, without even a smile, says,
"Okay. We've got another drop mission to make in support
of Wingate's Raiders. You guys know the pitch. They expect
you over the DZ (drop zone) at 0615 tomorrow."

There's nothing exactly new about that pitch, but the tone
of your commander's voice is different, so different that you
ask, "What's the cargo this time?"

"Mules," he answers, and stalks away.

"Mules," you repeat. "He must be kidding."

You make out your flight clearance and go to your airplane while they load it with . . . sure enough, jackasses.
Each animal has a parachute strapped to its back. You wonder if you're going to have any trouble getting rid of this
cargo when you get to the DZ.

A pilot from the old 315th Squadron, Captain Frank
Sweeney, who took part in one of these strange missions,
told how he handled a difficult problem with the animals:

"Since we had the mission to perform, we became interested in a few problems we thought would never concern us
as Air Force pilots. What kind of parachutes should we use
on a jackass? Since we would be at low altitude and in
rough air, how would we keep those animals quiet? How

would we get a balky jackass out the door? After being
dropped, would they land safely or would they break their
legs and have to be shot?

"With an assist from the medics, we doped the animals to
quiet them, loaded them aboard and headed deep into
Burma behind the Japanese lines. When we got to the drop
zone we got four of the animals out of the airplane in four
passes without any trouble. But the fifth one gave us
trouble.

"Apparently the dope had worn off this particular jackass,
who seemed thoroughly aware of what we were about to do
to him. As we led him to the door, he began to resist. When
he found his head sticking outside the door and into the
slipstream, he got panicky. When we tried to push him, he
did what all jackasses do—he promptly dug in with all four
feet and dared us to dislodge him.

"The handlers pushed and shoved while I made trip after
trip over the DZ flicking the 'jump' switch. Time after time it
was the same—they couldn't get the critter out.

"Exasperated, I turned the airplane over to the copilot and
went back to see what I could do about the situation. There
were the four handlers, the crew chief, and radio operator
standing completely baffled by this stubborn mule. The animal was standing facing the door, all four feet firmly
braced.

"We held a conference and finally hit on an idea. It
looked like what this animal needed was a little stimulus of
some sort applied from behind which would make him decide
that going through the door was the least of his troubles. The
only thing we could think of was to build a fire under him
but this could be dangerous.

"There was one kind of fire that might work, however.
Next time, my copilot got us over the DZ, I took out my
Zippo lighter, fired it up, raised the mule's tail and applied
the flame to the tender spot. The mule quivered for a
moment, suddenly came to life and leaped out the door into

the slipstream like a cannonball. That's the last we ever saw of him."

Although the C-47 was designed primarily for hauling people and bulky cargo, its use for other missions seemed unlimited. It was a "natural" for flying mercy missions to haul in food and medical supplies to front-line troops and to evacuate sick or wounded to rear-area hospitals. During World War II a C-47 flew one of the strangest missions ever recorded and it wasn't an overload mission. In fact, the cargo weighed less than a hundred pounds. Based on other flights which have been given names such as "Fireball Express," "Redball Express," and so on, this mission became known as the "Lipstick Express."

Colonel Frank MacNees, commander of the 435th Troop Carrier Group stationed in England, was standing with his back to the door when the young lieutenant entered. His eyes scanned the map on the wall in front of him. Without turning around, he brushed a hand through his silver hair, took a pencil from his breast pocket and marked a small red dot on the map.

"Take a look at this spot, Lieutenant," he said. "This is your drop zone for a 'special' I've got for you tonight."

The lieutenant shifted nervously and asked, "What's it this time, Colonel?'

"Son, I want you to drop a case of lipstick at this point."

"I don't want to seem insubordinate, Colonel," the young man said, "but don't you think there are more important things to drop than lipstick. This is the craziest cargo I ever heard of."

"Perhaps," the colonel replied, "but it has to be done. It won't be an easy flight for you, but I believe I have a route planned that will keep you out of most of Jerry's ack-ack all the way there and back. Now, here's where you'll find the heaviest gun concentrations. Follow me closely."

MacNees drew several red circles on the map and then

zigzagged a line around them from the base in England to the small red dot—the drop zone.

"From what Intelligence has told me," he continued, "these circles show where the most flak is concentrated. Naturally, these should be avoided by any aircraft, but especially by a C-47. They could knock you down in a second. You'll have to dogleg it there and back as I have drawn it here. If you try to fly a direct course, we'll be referring to you around here in the past tense. Got it?"

"Yes, Colonel, but . . . lipstick! What's so important that I have to stick my neck out for a case of lipstick? Whose idea was this?"

"I've given you your orders, Lieutenant. Follow the route I gave you and you shouldn't have any trouble."

"But, Colonel. . . ."

"Good luck to you, son. Now don't waste any more time. You've got a mission to fly."

The lieutenant's face turned beet red. He flipped the Colonel a halfhearted salute and strode from the room.

Colonel MacNees didn't blame the boy for being irritated about this particular flight because, in the face of it, it did seem ridiculous to be flying a case of lipstick to the front lines at night. The boy was a good pilot and a brave one and maybe he had a right to ask the why of the mission. But MacNees couldn't tell him the purpose of the lipstick because, if the boy knew how important it was and what it was to be used for, he might take every possible short cut and probably would be shot down before he could get very far. The Germans would like nothing better than to "zero in" on a lone C-47 transport.

MacNees sat down at his desk and studied the operations orders for the next day. He heard the familiar sound of a C-47's engines kicking over and roaring into life, then the sound of the engines pulling the airplane out into take-off position. There was a brief warmup, and then he listened as the familiar roar told him the C-47 was making its way into the night sky and toward the coast of France.

On the plane, the lieutenant, after he had leveled off, asked the navigator to come forward. "Take a look at the course the Old Man plotted and then give me a shorter one to fly," he said. "If we cut a few corners we'll cut quite a bit off the flying time of this mission."

"Yeah," the navigator nodded. "If the Old Man says there are flak batteries where he put these circles, I think he's wrong. I was over this same route three days ago, and we didn't get a single burst out of any of these places."

A few minutes later the navigator shouted a new heading to the pilot which would straighten out one of the doglegs the colonel had zigzagged on the map. The pilot nodded and swung the transport gently to the new heading.

Without warning, as they throbbed along, flares suddenly looped up into the dark sky like Fourth of July fireworks. The lights broke over their craft with such blinding brightness that the pilot didn't need a flashlight to see his map. The airplane rocked as heavy black flak followed the flares and the pilot struggled desperately to keep the plane level.

The crew chief came stumbling forward, trying to keep his balance.

"Sir, we've been hit! There must be a thousand holes in the fuselage! Does she fly all right?"

The young pilot nodded affirmatively, but was in no mood to answer questions. He shouted to the navigator, "Give me a new heading away from this stuff!'

The navigator handed him a new course and in a few minutes the flak stopped and the flares were gone. They cruised on unmolested and the crew relaxed from the few seconds of deadly tension.

The pilot flexed his fingers and let the copilot fly the airplane. "We just about had it that time," he said. "Maybe the Old Man knew what he was talking about, after all." The copilot nodded in silent agreement.

The C-47, though riddled with holes and slowed down by the disturbed air flow over her wings, somehow reached the target area. The pilot made two passes over the drop zone for identification and saw the Aldis lamp signal which marked the spot where he was to drop his strange cargo. The crew chief kicked the box out on signal, and the pilot turned the nose of the airplane toward England. He carefully followed the mapped route and inched the plane out of enemy territory between the danger areas like an infantryman picking his way through a mine field. German ack-ack batteries fired on the C-47 several times, but it was only token firing and didn't come too close.

As they passed over the Channel and the pilot knew they were safe, he began to think about the mission and the strange cargo of lipstick. The more he thought about it the more temper welled up inside him. A crew could be killed on a mission like this. And for what? A case of lipstick. What a waste of time and money—and men! What idiot had dreamed up a mission like this, anyhow?

By the time he parked the airplane the young pilot was furious. He paused a moment to look at the myriad of holes that had been stitched all over the fuselage of his C-47. He then hailed a passing jeep. "Take me to the CO's quarters," he shouted to the driver.

When the jeep stopped in front of the colonel's quarters the young officer leaped out, ran to the door and knocked loudly. Colonel MacNees hadn't retired yet. He couldn't go to sleep and forget the war when any of his boys were still in the air. He had stayed awake until he knew that the lieutenant had returned safely.

When MacNees opened the door, the pilot stomped past him and went inside.

"Colonel, I think you owe me an explanation about that stupid lipstick. We darn near got our fannies shot off over there and we're lucky we made it back. The airplane is full of holes and won't be safe to fly for quite a while. I just can't see how dropping lipstick to a bunch of Wacs will shorten the war!"

"Did you drop the case on the target?" the colonel asked.

"Right on the nose, but. . . ."

"Did you fly the course I gave you?"

"Not at first, I didn't. I changed, though, after the flak hit us."

"I gave you credit for being able to follow orders better than that, Lieutenant. If you had followed the course I gave you, you wouldn't have 'darn near got your fanny shot off.' Didn't you trust the course I gave you? What do you think we have Intelligence for?

"If you'll just settle down and cool off a bit maybe I can explain it to you—if you're willing to listen to me for a change." Colonel MacNees's calm and low voice continued. "You know, Lieutenant, sometimes it isn't always best to know at the time why we fly some of these missions. You no doubt remember the expression, 'Ours is not to reason why.' I certainly don't intend to hold that over your head, son, but sometimes it's just best that we go ahead and fly some of the so-called 'stupid' missions without knowing exactly why we're doing it.

"But now that you're back, I'm going to tell you about that lipstick. First of all, Lieutenant, you should know without my telling you that there are no Wacs in a combat zone. There were men below you at that drop zone—desperate, weary, scared, wounded, brave men. Right where you made your drop there are several hundred badly wounded men who were waiting for you to drop that 'stupid' lipstick."

"I don't understand all this, Colonel. It still doesn't fit."

"Maybe you don't know how lipstick is used on wounded men," the colonel continued. The lieutenant shook his head that he didn't. "Well, I'll tell you. When there are casualties in the front lines the medics rush in and quickly check them over to see the extent of their wounds. They then separate the more serious cases from the less serious ones and they have to have some way of marking the emergency cases for priority attention. The medics, having identified the emergencies, can have these cases rushed out to a field hospital immediately and send the less serious ones later.

"That lipstick, Lieutenant, that you fumed so much about

is being used at this very moment to mark the foreheads of seriously wounded men to distinguish the serious cases from those that can wait just a little longer for a doctor's care. That lipstick is actually saving lives tonight because it's the best thing ever invented for the job. They were out of it and you dropped it right into their laps. Believe me, son, there are a lot of mothers somewhere tonight who will see their sons come home from war because of that case of lipstick!"

The young lieutenant started to say something—to apologize—but the words wouldn't form. MacNees smiled, put his arm around the lad's shoulder and led him to the door.

"You'd better get some sleep," MacNees said. "More flying tomorrow."

The pilot walked out of the shack into the darkness with head bowed. MacNees called to him, "Say, son, I'm proud of the job you did tonight!"

Those words from the Old Man meant more than the Air Medal he had just earned for that flight.

Of all the overload stories that are told about the Gooney Bird, the one about a mission during the early days of the Berlin airlift seems to outweigh them all. Someone was almost responsible for clobbering a Gooney Bird and its crew just because he didn't understand the different meanings of "PAP" and "PSP."

Within a few hours after the Russians had barricaded the roads and railroads leading into Berlin in 1948, a lone C-47 winged through the air corridor from Wiesbaden, loaded with vital medical supplies. The Russians had blocked all ground transportation because of "technical difficulties" but they could not put up a barrier to the air corridors linking West Germany with Berlin short of starting a shooting war. Was this to be the beginning of World War III? No one knew.

The lone C-47 made it safely through, followed by many others, and the Berlin airlift, or "Operation Vittles," was born.

Within four days every available C-47 within flying distance of Wiesbaden was placed under the command of the Commanding General of the United States Air Forces in Europe, General Curtis E. LeMay, for temporary duty. Ninety-eight C-47s showed up, most of them from the 60th Troop Carrier Group, which had won battle stars in Algeria, French Morocco, Sicily, and Italy. It had been selected as the lone Troop Carrier Group to "occupy" Germany, and the airlift was a tailor-made job for it.

The first few flights into Berlin broke the ice. Desk pilots became airline pilots. Colonels, majors, and all officer ranks below, in fact, flew the airplanes. LeMay himself, cigar in hand, flew his share of missions to see for himself what problems his pilots would have. In some cases colonels flew as copilots for lieutenants because the lieutenants had more experience in the Gooney Bird. Everyone waited for the Russians to yell uncle after a week or so and let ground traffic resume. But the Russians were confident that no city could be kept alive solely by air. The three Allied zones of the partitioned city would be starved into submission.

After a week there was no letup. The cargoes changed from medical supplies to badly needed foodstuffs. Then it became a task of hauling in everything needed to keep the people of the city alive. The Gooney Birds hauled coal, flour, potatoes, truck parts, fruit, milk, you name it. The crews became dirty, tired, and exhausted as the days wore on. Airplanes were beginning to wear out. Fighter pilots with little or no weather flying time were taken out of their squadrons to fly as copilots to the more experienced twin-engine boys, some of whom had no more than thirty or forty hours in the C-47 before the airlift began.

As it became apparent that the Russians had no intention of giving in, it was also evident that the fleet of C-47s that filled the air lanes into and out of Berlin could not carry the great amounts of cargo needed. More and larger airplanes would be needed. Another Douglas product—the 4-engined C-54 *Skymaster*—was the plane for this job. About a hundred were ordered from the Far East, Panama, Hawaii, and the States to replace the C-47s which had borne the load from the beginning.

Richard Malkin, in his book *Boxcars in the Sky,* said, "At the beginning of the airlift 85 per cent of the aircraft were war-weary C-47s, averaging more than 3,000 hours per aircraft prior to Operation Vittles. Lack of parts and qualified ground crewmen created almost insurmountable obstacles, but during this period the group maintained more than 65 per cent of its airplanes in commission. This is far above the average, considering the scope of the operation.

"The 60th accomplished an exceptional feat by averaging 7,000 pounds, loaded weight, per aircraft, when the average load is 6,000 for the C-47. This was made possible by reducing the gas load. At times the planes were carrying up to an 8,000-pound payload."

One day just before the C-54 *Skymasters* took over the airlift, a C-47 pilot checked his load manifest sheet, nodded his satisfaction and went across the ramp to board his airplane. Looking briefly at the cargo, he muttered, "Another load of pierced aluminum planking for the Tegel Strip. I wonder how many hunks of this stuff it takes to lay that strip?"

He picked his way over the cargo to the cockpit, started the engines and ambled the Gooney Bird slowly, almost groggily, down the taxi strip to take-off position. The instruments showed that everything was functioning properly, but the plane seemed to need more power than usual just to taxi. He lined up for take-off and gave both engines all the power they could master. The plane moved slowly down the runway. At last the tail came up and with great effort the C-47 staggered off the ground just before she reached the end of the 6000-foot strip.

The pilot climbed the plane, creaking and groaning, to his assigned altitude and leveled off. Cowl flaps were closed and power adjusted on both engines. The air speed immediately sank to 110 miles per hour, about 30 below normal cruise. It wasn't a dangerous air speed, but something had to be wrong to drag it that low.

The pilot and copilot went over the check list again, visually checking to make sure that the landing gear and flaps were up. Finally the skipper settled back in his seat wearily and mumbled, "I guess she's just tired like I am."

When Berlin appeared on the horizon after more than the usual en route time had elapsed, the pilot entered the traffic pattern and made his approach. The air speed dropped dangerously when the landing gear was put down. Almost full power was needed to hold a safe air speed without stalling. The main wheels banged down on the runway with a jarring crunch and, at the same time, the tail wheel blasted to earth with a thud that rocked the airplane its full length. As the puzzled pilot taxied to the ramp he knew that something was wrong. No Gooney Bird he had ever flown before had seemed less anxious to fly than this one.

Before he opened the door he reasoned he'd better check the load before the German workers swarmed over it. He looked at the load manifest again and it showed clearly the letters "PAP" for "Pierced Aluminum Planking." Bending down, he fingered one of the planks, straightened up with surprise and yelled, "Hey! This isn't aluminum, it's *steel!*"

It *was* steel planking—Pierced Steel Planking (PSP)—and the pilot had good reason to yell. Instead of the aluminum, he had carried a load of steel that weighed 13,500 pounds— about twice the weight any C-47 ought to carry!

The next year after the Berlin airlift ended, the Gooney Bird was to fly and fight in a new war that would once more test its load-carrying capabilities and its role as the dependable old work horse. This time the place was called Korea, to engage in a "police action," they said. The C-47s went there officially as the 21st Troop Carrier Squadron, but they soon dropped that identity and called themselves the Kyushu Gypsies, because after the Communist forces surged across the 38th parallel, they had no permanent home.

When United Nations forces were mustered, Greek and Thai pilots brought in several C-47s to augment the Gypsy Squadron and flew as an integral part of that unit. The three C-47s that winged in from Thailand had their original engines. Since no records were kept, it was impossible to tell how many flying hours each had amassed. Baling wire and coat hangers had long since replaced cotter pins and safety wire, and even the control cables had been patched with pieces of baling wire. Over the years mud daubers had built nests inside the engine cowlings, and they were still intact. Most of the instruments were either inoperative or missing entirely from the panel, and the fabric covering the tail surfaces and the ailerons was held together with Scotch tape and adhesive plaster.

The exploits of the Gypsies would fill scores of books, but of all the missions they flew, one operation stands out in their minds as giving them the most pride and satisfaction—not only in their unit but in the plane they flew. It was an operation that the U. S. Marines would not forget either.

The weather was frigid as the cold air and clouds pushed in on the peninsula battleground and on Japan. Emergency messages came in, saying that some C-47s were needed at Hamhung to evacuate wounded marines out of the village of Hagaru-ri near the Chosen Reservoir. The 1st Marine Regiment had been cut off and other Marine and Army units had concentrated their survivors at Hagaru-ri. On November 30 the first C-47s departed for Hamhung Airfield. By the end of the day thirteen C-47s sat on the Hamhung airfield ready to work. The next day the planes took off for Hagaru-ri, passing through a saddleback ridge on the way, looking beyond to Koto-ri and the winding little road that led across the valley to the Chosen Reservoir.

Midway between the two towns the pilots saw a convoy stretched along the road. They wondered how this could be if the Chinese had the American marines encircled. They looked closer. The convoy was not moving. It had been attacked, gutted and destroyed. There was no sign of life around the ruined trucks and tanks.

The airstrip at Hagaru-ri was only 2,500 feet long, hardly long enough to operate from safely and easily with no load, let alone taking in supplies and bringing out wounded. Each landing was what pilots call a "short field landing."

On the ground and out of their planes, the crews of the C-47s saw more indications of battle. They smelled the stench of men's wounds, of unwashed bodies. They saw the weapons and small fires where the men were huddling to keep warm. They heard the nasty barking of rifles, the chattering of machine-gun fire, and heavy blasts of artillery close by.

The marines began loading the stretchers of the seriously wounded into the C-47s immediately. Others not so seriously injured walked by themselves. Several hobbled on canes and crutches made from branches of trees. To a man they moved quietly and with discipline.

One of the first C-47s into Hagaru-ri that day was hit by bullets from small-arms fire on the ground. Major Paul Fritz, one of the pilots, later said they flew so low over the enemy that it was a wonder he couldn't knock the airplanes down with rocks.

As they were getting ready for take-off, a young marine told Fritz, "It's nice of you to come and get these fellows. Some of them are pretty badly hurt."

"You're welcome," Fritz answered, knowing that this reply sounded strange.

The young marine continued, "Tomorrow we're going to convoy out, soon as you Air Force people get the wounded out."

Fritz didn't have the heart to tell him that the convoy they were expecting would never arrive.

As far as load limits were concerned, few Gypsy pilots paid any attention to them at Hagaru-ri. A pilot would take all the wounded he could load into his plane. One crew brought out thirty-eight, but this number was challenged by another crew who boasted they had brought out forty. Fritz's crew did better than that. As they loaded the fortieth man, Fritz looked back at the truck where two more badly wounded marines waited quietly. Their faces were set in agony. Fritz looked inside his plane. There was still some floor space; so he motioned to the crew to make way for two more.

When Fritz had first flown to Hagaru-ri, he hit a bump near the end of the strip that had not been smoothed away. Fritz, like others who had hit the bump and bounced roughly, wasn't too happy about it. Now he faced the prospect of taking off an extremely heavy plane loaded with wounded men. What about that bump? he wondered.

Chugging along laboriously, Fritz's plane couldn't seem to decide whether or not it was going to fly. As Fritz neared the bump, he cringed when he saw it about to pass under the nose of his plane. The Gooney Bird slammed into the bump and at that instant Fritz hauled back on the wheel. The plane bounced into the air, shuddered for an instant but miraculously continued to fly. Fritz sank back in his seat, sweat beading his forehead in the cold cockpit. Thanks to the bump he had previously sworn at, the old Gooney Bird had been pitched into flight.

The day after Fritz's encounter with the runway bump, another pilot wasn't quite so fortunate. On his take-off run, the pilot seemed to be gaining flying speed without effort, when suddenly the tail of the airplane settled and the airplane flew dizzily upward. Seconds later it stalled, plummeted to the ground, slashed its way through several small trees, and then stopped.

Fortunately no one was injured, however, the plane had crashed in no man's land near the firmly entrenched enemy. Two Air Force fighter pilots flying overhead saw the crash. They watched the passengers stream from the wrecked Gooney Bird and try to hobble away. Streaking out of the sky, the twin fighters dived on the enemy snipers and held them off until the marines were rescued.

The C-47, for all practical purposes, was destroyed, but the fighter pilots wanted to make certain that it was not captured later by the Communists and put into service. Again they streaked in, machine-gunning the Gooney Bird on the ground. Bullets hit the gas tanks and the plane exploded in a ball of fire. To the C-47 pilots who had to watch the destruction of one of their planes, it was a sickening sight.

After five days of operations at Hagaru-ri, the C-47 crews could see their efforts paying off. The marines could now concentrate on holding off the ever-tightening enemy ring instead of caring for the wounded. The daily crop of casualties decreased, and those who still fought were well supplied with warm clothing, food, and ammunition brought in by the C-47s. But it was time for the marines to fight their way to the coast. "The way out is the way through," one marine said.

On the sixth day, as the Gooney Birds went into Hagaru-ri, the advance spearhead of the encircled Marine division was already inching its way forward on the only road that existed. Tanks spearheaded the infantrymen as they leap-frogged from one fire-fight position to the next. Small detachments of men scouted the flanks of the main body, and a handful of vehicles labored a short distance behind. The semblance of security they had had before in their small defense perimeter vanished. Now they were completely vulnerable and tired. The Siberian winter gave no respite, no quarter, but the marines were on their way.

By noon of that day it was time to give the airstrip back to the Chinese. A C-47 which had been damaged beyond repair on the field was blown up by a hand grenade.

But the Americans still were not finished. Someone decided that a new airstrip should be bulldozed out at Koto-ri near where the Marine division would pass. This was done, and what a strip it was. Hagaru-ri had been short, but the Koto-ri strip was only 2,000 feet long. As soon as it was finished, Gooney Birds landed every few minutes and supplied the marines for two more days. The Gypsy planes, plus some airplanes borrowed from some other U.N. units for the Chosen Reservoir operation, had hauled in 547,000 pounds of supplies and ammunition to the marines. On the trips out they had evacuated 4,638 men. Two C-47s were lost, but not a single flight crewman lost his life or was even seriously injured.

Several days after Christmas, the Kyushu Gypsy aircrews who had participated in the marine evacuation were standing in formation while a glowing tribute to them was being read over the loud-speaker system. Men were decorated with Distinguished Flying Crosses and Air Medals. Behind them in a precise line sat the tired, weary C-47s that needed new tires, new engines, and new face liftings. As the unit commander pinned a D.F.C. on one pilot and congratulated him, the pilot replied, "Thank you, sir, but I don't deserve it. It's these airplanes here that should get the medals. Without them, no one could have done the job. With them, anyone could."

In the desperate days of the Pusan Perimeter fighting when the United Nations forces were trying to maintain a toehold on the Korean peninsula, logisticians of the three services were at their wit's end trying to smooth out the delivery of priority air freight destined for the front lines. Cargo was delivered by four-engined planes to the Tachikawa Air Base warehouse in Japan from the United States where it was classified and stacked to await delivery. When transport planes were available, the badly-needed war matériel was flown to Ashiya, in southwest Japan, the temporary home of the Kyushu Gypsies. From there the Gypsies flew it to the Pusan Perimeter in C-47s.

In those confused days, an independent communications system was connected directly to the command post in Pusan. Priorities for the supplies were established and the Gypsy Squadron notified. The squadron supply officer would earmark the matériel on hand and deliver it according to the priority given.

One day the Gypsy Squadron commander received a call saying that thousands of pounds of graham crackers were required in Pusan with the highest priority. This strange request was relayed to Tokyo, and all other shipments were put aside while hundreds of cases of the crackers were located and flown to Pusan.

Within a few days graham crackers piled up at all the bases in Japan. They piled higher and higher at Ashiya as the C-47s could not deliver them to Pusan fast enough. The

Gypsies even took their airplanes out of the hangars to make room for storing graham crackers.

Then the crackers began to pile up at the supply point in Taegu, Korea, and soon there was a stack as high as a two-story building. Supply officers on the scene, mystified as to why boxes of the dry-brown crackers had suddenly taken priority over ammunition and medical supplies, tried to shut off the stream.

When the operation was about 50 per cent complete, the graham crackers were stacked high at Tachikawa, Ashiya, and Taegu, priorities were suddenly changed and the Gypsies started hauling 3.5-inch bazooka shells as fast as they could move them. The graham crackers were suddenly forgotten in the excitement of war and became, for a time, one of the Far East's unsolved mysteries.

Many of the Kyushu Gypsies thought the South Korean Army had run out of staple food and needed graham crackers to supplement their usual diet. But this explanation was unsatisfactory, because the crackers never reached the front lines.

One evening a few weeks after this strange happening Colonel Troy Crawford, commander of the Kyushu Gypsy Squadron, overheard a conversation between two Army officers in the Tachikawa Officers Club. They were discussing graham crackers and seemed to be quite amused. Crawford questioned them and persuaded them to divulge the highly secret information that the graham cracker incident was the result of a curious mixture of coded and uncoded messages.

Large quantities of bazookas had been shipped to Korea for use against the enemy tanks at Pusan. The United Nations troops, running low on bazooka ammunition, had called for resupply with the highest priority. Except during extreme emergencies, code was always used in communications between Korea and Japan. This time the urgency was so great that the Army communications men transmitted the message in the clear with the exception of the name of the needed item. The code word for bazooka ammunition the day of this message had been *graham crackers!*

What no other airplane can do

6

Give me fifty DC-3's and the Japanese can have the Burma Road.

—CHIANG KAI-SHEK

OF ALL THE ATTRIBUTES of the Douglas DC-3/C-47, the one most comforting to pilots is its ability to fly on one engine. While many pilots have had to find out about this the hard way, including both of the authors of this book, the record for distance with only one propeller turning belongs to Major "Skip" Kimball, of the U. S. Marines. Kimball was a member of SCAT—South Pacific Combat Air Transport Group—and was slated to fly a load of cargo in a C-47 from Pearl Harbor to San Diego.

At the halfway point between Hawaii and the States— nicknamed "Jones Corner"—Kimball lost power on his left engine and had to feather it. Since the distance was the same either way and the wind was 70 degrees to his course, the choice of whether to turn back to Hawaii or continue on to the States was academic. What mattered was how far the C-47 could fly on one engine.

With the heavy load, it soon became apparent that the Gooney Bird could not maintain its altitude unless he jettisoned some of his cargo. The crew kicked the boxes overboard, the airplane picked up speed with one engine, and Major Kimball lumbered into San Diego without further mishap. He had set a record by flying the C-47 more than 1,100 miles with only one propeller turning!

The second longest distance ever flown on a single engine by a twin-engined plane is claimed by Commander Frank E. Kimberling, U.S.N., in a ski-equipped R4D-8, a Super DC-3 (naturally called the "Super-Gooney"), in September of 1958. Kimberling was to fly his plane, equipped with long-range tanks, from Quonset Point, Rhode Island, to Antarctica via San Francisco, Hawaii, Canton Island, the Fijis, and New Zealand.

Kimberling's nonstop flight from Quonset to San Francisco was uneventful, but the leg to Hawaii presaged the difficulty he was to have later on the trip. Three times he left San Francisco for Hawaii. Three times he got 500 miles over the Pacific and had to return for a new engine. He finally made it after 14 hours 45 minutes of uneventful and wearying flight.

Loaded with approximately 10,000 pounds of cargo for Antarctic operations, plus an extra 500 gallons of gas in fuselage tanks, Kimberling blasted off the runway at Honolulu with the aid of fifteen JATO (Jet-assisted Take-off) bottles. The time was 6:35 P.M., September 29, 1958. The distance to Canton atoll in the Phoenix Islands was 1,670 miles.

All was serene as Kimberling, his two copilots, Lt. Reginald Simmons and Lt. (jg) Norman Davis, plus seven other crew members, settled down for the long flight. At fifteen minutes after midnight, with 620 miles to go, the hours of boredom were interrupted by the terrorizing whine of the propeller on the left engine as it ran wild and caught fire. Kimberling immediately tried to feather the propeller but to no avail. The propeller speed governor was shot and if the engine could not be stopped, the whirling steel blade would come ripping through the fuselage like a buzz saw.

Nothing Kimberling did could bring the rpms of the engine down. The only thing left to do was to cut the fuel off and let the dead propeller windmill until it froze for lack of oil. The unfeathered propeller, however, would act as a tremendous drag on the plane, just as if a huge round steel plate were affixed to the plane in its place.

Kimberling had been cruising at 8,000 feet when the emergency occurred. Seconds later, by the time the gas had stopped flowing to the disabled engine, the plane was down to 1,000 feet and headed for the tops of the waves. The good engine was wide open and the plane was in a violent skid from the excessive weight and drag.

"Throw out everything that you can move!" Kimberling commanded.

Ten thousand pounds of cargo is a lot of weight to throw overboard, but the seven crewmen needed no prompting. To their dismay, the "jump door," a small door which can be drawn inside the plane in flight and replaced after a supply or paratroop drop, had been riveted shut. The only alternative was to rip the pins from the whole door and push it overboard, which they did. Unhappily, this extra drag, even with the whole cargo jettisoned, added to Kimberling's problem of keeping the plane flying.

Piece by piece, the entire 10,000 pounds of cargo was unceremoniously dragged to the yawning doorway and pushed out. Each pound dropped gave the crippled Super-Gooney and its human cargo a better chance to survive. The plane was now down to only 100 feet over the waves and was still descending.

"Throw out *everything*!" Kimberling commanded, and out went suitcases, radios, the radar set, navigation equipment, and tools. Lt. Norman Davis, fully realizing the urgency of the situation and energized by it, personally carried the six 280-pound JATO bottles to the doorway and dropped them out. Davis, who weighs less than 200 pounds, said later that he was so anxious to get them out that he didn't even think they were heavy at the time.

For the next six hours, Kimberling battled the drag created by the windmilling engine and the open doorway. He used full right rudder trim and he and his copilots took turns holding the right rudder all the way in with their feet. The airplane stayed in a skid at an air speed of 89 knots— barely above stalling. The radio operator, Mike Ortega, had flashed a Mayday message on the liaison radio set at the first sign of trouble. Although they were a thousand miles south of Hawaii, the first station to acknowledge was Argentia, Newfoundland. Next, Tokyo answered and flashed the word to Canton and around the Pacific.

Reaction was immediate. British RAF air-sea rescue aircraft were dispatched from Christmas Island and two U. S. Air Force planes departed from Pearl Harbor. In the meantime, Captain John Connelly, flying a QANTAS Super-G *Constellation* was just departing from Honolulu for the Fiji Islands. Flying at maximum cruise, Connelly finally caught up with the Super-Gooney 120 miles from Canton. As soon as Kimberling spotted the *Constellation* he radioed: "We expect to run out of gas ten minutes out of Canton."

Connelly acknowledged the transmission and relayed the message to Canton atoll. There, a rescue boat was dispatched—an 8-foot rowboat powered by an outboard motor and manned by a lone Fiji Islander. At thirteen miles out, Kimberling figured he had only twenty gallons of gas left. Five miles out, the gas gauge read "Empty."

"I'll never know how we made that last five miles," Commander Kimberling says, "but we did. Just as the wheels touched down, the starboard engine sputtered and died. We had flown for five hours and forty-seven minutes under the most difficult drag conditions any pilot ever had to contend with to stay aloft. Believe me, I've flown lots of hours in lots

of planes and had my share of near misses. Of all the airplanes in the world, only the faithful Gooney Bird could
have done what we asked it to do that day!"

Kimberling's Super-Gooney didn't get to Antarctica that
year in time to participate in the Navy's Operation High
Jump. The next year, however, during an exploratory flight
over the Horlick Mountains, the plane's luck ran out and it
crashed but without loss of life. Today, Kimberling's Super
DC-3 lies buried beneath tons of Antarctic ice and snow.
Someday, if the world's aeronautical engineers give up and
decide that no replacement for a DC-3 can ever be produced, someone may resurrect Kimberling's plane and fly it
again.

On another occasion Major Owen Ross, a Marine pilot, was
500 miles from Espíritu Santo in the New Hebrides Islands
when one engine of his DC-3 stopped without warning and he
could not start it again. Unlike Kimball and Kimberling Ross
could not jettison his cargo, because he was carrying twenty
wounded marines—all stretcher cases—to a rear-area hospital.
Ross chugged along dreading what would happen if he lost
power on his good engine. He nursed his plane along carefully and finally brought it to a safe landing. Today there are
twenty marines whose lives once depended on one small,
spinning propeller of a DC transport.

When it comes to weight-lifting on one engine, Air Force
Captain J. G. Herring, who found himself 250 miles at sea
with a load weighing 29,000 pounds, takes the prize as far as
the authors can determine. He could have jettisoned the
cargo, but since he knew it was badly needed in combat he
refused to let any of it be tossed overboard. Instead, he kept
his cargo intact and flew tediously to his destination on one
engine, hampered occasionally by scattered cumulus cloud
buildups that made the air speed come dangerously near the
stall point.

Whenever a group of crew chiefs get together in a bull
session they cuss and discuss the experiences they have had

with the pilots with whom they fly, and the meeting would put a ladies' sewing circle to shame. Take the time when Sergeant Walter E. Jones told about a pilot who forgot how long the Gooney Bird's wings were. It is an excellent example of the luck and audacity of some pilots who had blind faith in the ability of the old Gooney Bird to fly under any circumstances. His story is repeated here in the same colorful words Jones used when he told it to the authors:

"In the late summer of 1944 I was a member of the 27th Transport Squadron of the 302nd Transport Wing, stationed at Heston Airdrome just a few miles outside London. Our wing had charge of all the ferrying of aircraft and the transport work in England.

"In September, after the breakout at Saint-Lô, we flew gasoline to General Patton before the Red Ball Express was set up. We also flew rockets, blood plasma and other critical items to France and took wounded men and PW's back to England on the return trips.

"The day I want to tell you about started like any other day. I was the flight engineer assigned to this C-47 and we were to take a load of high-ranking officers of some armored division to Metz, France. The trip over was uneventful until we landed at a strip that was made to accommodate a squadron of P-47 "Jugs." The strip was a common one for France at that time with steel matting runways, small taxi strips, and lots of tents. We landed just behind a flight of fighter planes, and my pilot, being unfamiliar with the layout of the field, started following them around the taxi strip. We didn't get very far. The strip was all right for the Jugs to taxi around on, but was much too narrow for the C-47. We hit both wing tips on some good-sized trees growing along the strip. The tail came up in the air and bounced down a couple of times as we came to a jolting halt. I ran back to open the door and get the ladder down and was almost trampled in the stampede of passengers trying to get out of the plane.

"After we had all piled out and looked the plane over, I was all for putting it on a red cross (making an X on the form with a red pencil to indicate that the plane was unsafe until the proper maintenance had been performed), pulling it over to one side and leaving it until some Service Squadron could come and fix it or cannibalize it for spare parts. I knew it would be beyond my capability to fix it, so all I wanted to do was get out of there on the next plane going back to our base.

"The left wing was turned up at about a 60-degree angle for about a foot and a half. The right one was torn and mangled from the nut plates on the wing all the way up to the tip and back to the last spar that holds the aileron on. It was a mess, to say the least, and I would have bet anything I had right then against a discharge that the C-47 wouldn't fly again until both wing tips and maybe both wings had been replaced.

"But the captain looked it all over and told me to get the crash axe from the ship. Then he got up on the right wing and started chopping all the torn metal away that used to be our right wing tip. He chopped off all that he could get at and then we got some mallets and hammers and beat the jagged ends back inside what were left on the tip. It was an awful-looking thing, with jagged metal sticking out all over. Then he used his pocket knife to cut off one piece of rubber deicer boot that was hanging down.

"Going over to the left wing, we beat and beat on that one trying to straighten it out, but we didn't do much good. The thing was still cocked up in the air about 60 degrees. We were tired of pounding on it. It was then that the captain told me we were going to fly it back to Heston. Well, you can imagine what I felt like telling him; but I was young and foolish, so we piled in and taxied to the Operations tent. He told them he was going to take off in spite of the accident we had just had, and filed his flight clearance.

"As I was pulling the ladder up, a commander from the Royal Navy came running up puffing like an old ferryboat. He wanted a lift back to England and had just heard we were leaving. What a sailor was doing that far away from the ocean, only the King knew.

"I told him about our damage and pointed to the left wing tip, which looked like it was going to flap. He hesitated a minute, uttered a few 'Bless my souls,' then decided that if we were crazy enough to fly the ship that way, he was crazy enough to go with us.

"He was a rather portly man, to say the least, and we certainly had a time getting him strapped in a parachute. We finally made it, but he looked like a sack of potatoes, he was bulging so much from the chute straps.

"By the time we were at the end of the runway to take off, it looked as though every man at that base was there to see us kill ourselves trying to get that clobbered bird into the air.

"Well, sir, that old airplane took off and climbed like it was new. We climbed to about 7,000 feet and cruised at 130 miles per hour. I really expected to see that right aileron and the rest of the wing tip go at any second. I could see it fluttering and starting to bend. I told the pilot about it and he slowed down a little bit. The ship flew remarkably well, considering its condition. It required only about three degrees of aileron trim which we attributed to the left wing tip being bent up.

"When we landed at Heston and taxied up to Operations, I think all the brass in the United Kingdom was out there, wanting to know how many planes we had torn up taxiing into them. They could hardly believe we had flown that C-47 in that condition from Metz, France, to London in one piece.

"In our excitement over the trip, we had completely forgotten about the commander. I found him stretched out under a couple of blankets fast asleep. It's wonderful what ignorance will do sometimes. Our predicament didn't worry him a bit. He got up, stretched, thanked me and plumped down the ladder just like he was getting off a streetcar after a day at the office.

"When we got the C-47 back into the shops and started to change wing tips, we could see how lucky we really were. That last spar and one aileron mounting bracket had been cracked. Another quarter of an inch and we would have had to change the whole wing because it would have ripped all the nut plates out that fasten the wing tip to the wing.

"I often think back on that day and I wouldn't do it again even if I could be Chief of Staff of the Air Force. I've just gotten smarter, I guess.

"I've long since graduated from C-47s but will always have a soft spot in my heart for the best airplane ever built and will always remember my association with it. No one will ever be able to tell me that another airplane can be as forgiving. I *know!*"

Captain Jack Farris, pilot of the "Geronimo," was a man who resented being assigned to fly the Gooney Bird. He had wanted to fly fighters, but had been sent to C-47 transition school and then to England after graduating from flying training. Almost every day since getting his wings, Farris had been the victim of routine, or so it seemed to him. He called his job "boring," even though many times he had been shot at as he groped his way dangerously low over the German antiaircraft installations.

The top brass had told the C-47 Troop Carrier pilots that their job was just as important as the work of the bombers and fighters, but hauling troops and cargo didn't seem to be a fair shake when the pilots who could shoot back at the enemy or dump bombs on his factories were getting all the glory and most of the big medals. Other than intercepting occasional small-arms or ack-ack ground fire, Farris had not been in actual fighting. It wasn't that he wanted to be shot at, hit by flak, or have to bail out as a result of battle, he simply wasn't happy about flying an airplane that couldn't defend itself.

Back at the base Farris listened to the fighter and bomber boys telling how they had been hit by flak or how someone had been shot down by an enemy plane. Their enthusiasm for combat was contagious and he wanted a P-51 or P-47 so badly he dreamed about it. He felt that he himself had con-

A single C-47, towing two CG-4A gliders, takes off from a 9th Troop Carrier Command air base somewhere in France, March 1945. (U.S. Air Force photo)

On February 13, 1943, an Air Force pilot won the Distinguished Flying Cross for flying this C-47 with a spare wing strapped under its belly to a distant airstrip. A sister ship needed it to be made flyable again. This C-47 was flown 285 miles to an advanced air base where the damaged plane was repaired. Later in the war, B-25 and P-40 wings were often transported in this manner.

(Douglas Aircraft Co. photo)

This amphibious version of the C-47 proved the Gooney Bird's versatility. In spite of the drastic external changes, the flying characteristics were not altered appreciably. The pontoons were 41 feet long with a series of watertight bulkheads. Extra space in the floats was used for gasoline.

(Douglas Aircraft Co. photo)

Soaring noiselessly at the end of a tow rope is the XCG-17 being towed by a Consolidated B-24 during tests at Wright Field, Ohio. With its 14-to-1 glide ratio, it could outglide the best combat glider of the war, the CG-4A, which had only a 12-to-1 glide ratio. (Douglas Aircraft Co. photo)

Close-up view of the XCG-17 showing how engine area was streamlined. The XCG-17s stalling speed was only 35 miles per hour, but it could be towed as fast as 290 miles per hour without structural damage. After tests, however, military authorities decided that the C-47 was too valuable with its engines and could not be spared as a glider. (Douglas Aircraft Co. photo)

The Russians have claimed the DC-3 as their own. Designated at first the PS-84, it was later called the Li-2 for its "inventor" Lissunov. Some Li-2s were outfitted with turret machine guns located in the navigator's astrodome position. Some were also equipped with wood-burning stoves for passenger comfort when flying in subzero temperatures. (U.S. Air Force photo)

It would be difficult to find anyone today who has not seen a Gooney Bird in flight. It has been estimated that the world's airlines have flown it more than 200 million miles in scheduled operations; no one dares to say how many miles it has been flown by military air forces or private owners. This classic photo was taken during World War II as a C-47 flies past the Pyramids of Egypt on a regular supply run.   (U.S. Air Force photo)

One of the many contraptions tried out on military Gooney Birds was this factory-style conveyor belt powered by a small electric motor. Its purpose was to enable a C-47 to discharge its cargo quickly. Extending from behind the pilot's compartment to the rear of the plane, the belt ran at the rate of about six feet per second. A 4,000-pound load could be dropped in about 60 seconds, thus enabling the unarmed plane to make a single pass and a quick getaway from the drop zone.　　　　　　　　　　　　　　　　　(U.S. Air Force photo)

The Gooney Bird has hauled just about anything that will fit into its fuselage. Here a tractor is being guided into a C-47 in the Pacific area for transport to an advanced airstrip. On the return flight, wounded soldiers were carried to rear area hospitals. (U.S. Air Force photo)

Probably the most reluctant passengers ever to board a C-47 were the mules transported in the China–Burma–India theater of operations. This one objects to being led aboard the plane. Mules were not only flown from point to point but some were actually dropped by parachute to units operating behind Japanese lines. (U.S. Air Force photo)

At a front line airstrip in Korea, Army medics load wounded soldiers aboard a C-47 of the Kyushu Gypsy Squadron. More than half of the 200,000 men evacuated from the combat zone were carried by the planes of this unit.

(U.S. Air Force photo)

A Navy R4D is shown blasting off the deck of the carrier USS Philippine Sea *in 1947 for operations in the Antarctic. Aboard was Admiral Richard E. Byrd, who was making his last visit to the frozen continent. The ski-wheel combination proved to be the best gear for operating in the snow. Note the elevator fins on the rear of each ski to stabilize it in flight.* (U.S. Navy photo)

While in level flight under instrument conditions, this C-47 flown by Major John A. Fowle and Captain E. P. Kelley inadvertently crashed into the side of Mount Fujiyama, March 7, 1956. The plane ground to a quick halt in the snow and the entire crew escaped injury except for a black eye suffered by Kelley.

(U.S. Air Force photo)

Another aviation "first" was scored by the Gooney Bird when the U.S. Navy's Que Sera Sera landed at the South Pole on October 31, 1956 shown here just as it touched down. The pilot on this flight was Commander Conrad "Gus" Shinn and copilot was Captain William "Trigger" Hawkes. The Gooney also claims the honor as the first aircraft to have been landed at both poles. (U.S. Navy photo)

After landing at the South Pole, dogs and supplies were unloaded from the R4D. The Navy maintains an airstrip at the South Pole year-round and conducts weather observations and experiments. (U.S. Navy photo)

This Air Force C-47 shown elevated on a mound of ice at Ice Station Bravo (also called T-3) in the Arctic Ocean had made a forced landing on the floating ice island and could not be flown out. The aircraft was "cannibalized" and only the shell remained on this wind-eroded mound of ice. Ice Station Bravo was used as a weather station and scientific research outpost by the Air Force from 1952 until 1961. Deactivation became necessary when a 2,500-foot runway began to break up and drift away. (U.S. Air Force photo)

A bomb planted in the baggage compartment of this airline DC-3 exploded while the plane was in flight. In spite of the damage, the pilot nursed it to a safe landing without injury to passengers or crew. (Douglas Aircraft Co. photo)

Three 7.62 rapid-firing mini-guns protrude from the fuselage of this AC-47 gunship at Nha Trang Air Base in South Vietnam. The use of the slow-flying Gooney Birds in a counter-insurgency role against ground targets thrust the ageless Gooney into still another mission for which it was not originally designed. (U.S. Air Force photo)

DC-3s have sustained heavy damage in flight and still managed to return safely. This airliner collided with an Arizona mountaintop in severe turbulence and lost several feet from its left wing tip. A safe landing was made at Phoenix by the pilot. (Photo by Joey Starr)

After World War II, the Douglas Company attempted to market an updated,
faster version of the DC-3. Wing tips and horizontal and vertical stabilizers were
squared off. Engine nacelles were streamlined, the wheels were covered with
fairing doors and the tail wheel was retracted. Speed was increased to about 200
mph with a payload of 30 passengers.   (Douglas Aircraft Co. photo)

As if proof were needed that the DC-3 will never fade away, this is the latest
updating in the plane's long history of modernization. It is the Tri Turbo Three
with three Pratt & Whitney PT-6 engines installed. Outboard wing tanks provide
a range of 3,000 miles, making it possible for the Tri Turbo Three to take off and
climb to 10,000 feet cruising altitude, and with the center engine feathered,
fly a 3,000-mile mission and still have one hour of fuel remaining. Cruise
speed is 230 mph.   (Photo from Jack Conroy, the plane's "manufacturer")

The idea of using turboprops to replace the piston engines was originally tried on two British European Airways DC-3s in 1951. The cabin was not pressurized. At the high altitudes that were possible because of the jet engines, BEA found that they could not carry bottled goods, fruits or livestock safely.

(British European Airways photo)

H. L. "Smokey" Stover knows what to do with a surplus Gooney Bird he rescued from the Air Force's "boneyard." He made it into a mobile home by mounting the fuselage, sans empennage and wings, on a truck frame and installing a Lincoln engine. Other DC-3s have found uses as a chicken coop, coffee house, playground equipment, a restaurant and storage sheds after being grounded permanently in various parts of the world. (Los Angeles Times photo)

The DC-2 shown here, formerly used as a fighter-bomber by the Finnish Air Force, is now a coffee house in Hameenlinna, Finland. (Finnish Air Force photo)

This Varig Air Lines DC-3 is now a prime attraction in a park in Rio de Janeiro, Brazil. (Douglas Aircraft Co. photo)

More than 10,000 DC-3s/C-47s were turned out by the Douglas Aircraft Co. before production ceased in 1945. A production line system, similar to that used for auto production, was instituted as shown here at the company's Santa Monica plant. About 2,000 of these aircraft are believed still flying today.

(Douglas Aircraft Co. photo)

The Remmert-Werner Co. of St. Louis and other firms specialized in renovating Gooney Birds for private owners. This one had been abandoned and turned into a chicken coop by an Alabama farmer. Using parts of other DC-3s, the Remmert-Werner Co. rebuilt it into a plush plane for the executives of a large corporation who are unaware of its former status.   (Remmert-Werner photo)

The uses to which the Gooney can be put seems endless. Here a "dung-carrying Dakota" is being loaded in New Zealand. The fertilizer is dropped on crops and spread by the blast of the propellers. Of all the planes tried, the DC-3 has proven to be best. Besides the load of "topdressing," the pilot carries his small Fiat along in the aft fuselage.

(Photo by Fred Tomlinson)

tributed little to the war effort, although he had dropped paratroopers behind enemy lines, hauled ammunition and supplies when men were surrounded and desperate, and even dropped agents to work with the French Resistance Forces. But this knowledge didn't lessen the monotony he felt flying his "milk runs."

One night Farris was in for the surprise of his life. He checked his load of paratroopers, climbed into "Geronimo," and took off for France with a formation of other C-47s. Nothing happened during the first part of the flight—not until he neared the drop zone on the southern coast of France. Then all hell broke loose.

An enemy ack-ack shell tore through the fuselage on the starboard side, ripping a six-foot hole. A fragment split the aluminum and damaged every rib from the new bulkhead to the vertical stabilizer. It passed through the airplane, ripped off the door, and killed a paratrooper sitting next to the door. Then a second burst hit the plane and carried away a portion of the rudder. The explosion also blew away a large box of equipment inside the fuselage. The impact was so great that Farris said it felt like one of the engines had come crashing into the pilot's compartment.

The copilot, Captain Joseph Baxter, went back to survey the damage, and what he saw knotted his stomach. Only the front half of the airplane was intact. The aft section was a sieve of jagged holes. There were so many holes in the fuselage that the wind whistling through them slowed the C-47 to 110 miles per hour. Wounded and dead paratroopers were spilled all over the aisle. Farris and Baxter knew what they had to do. Farris rolled the Gooney Bird over on one wing to make a sharp turn, and then, leveling off, he headed for Africa, alone and vulnerable. He fire-walled both throttles to use all the power he could squeeze from the engines. But he lost altitude steadily until he was almost skimming the waves of the Mediterranean. His instruments were useless and his only means of keeping the airplane right side up was to steer by the reflection of the moonlight on the water.

But Farris's number wasn't up that night. He fought the airplane all the way back across the Mediterranean to his base in North Africa. When he attempted to shut down the engines after landing, one of them was so hot that it continued to run even after the switch was shut off. The airplane never flew again. And never again did Farris complain that flying the Gooney Bird was boring.

Combat was not the only trial the Gooney Bird had to face during World War II. Flying in the frozen wastelands of the Far North had prospects which were just as harrowing.

The possibility of going down in the frozen wastes in places where it might be impossible for rescue crews to locate survivors was always present. Many airplanes with their crews had disappeared in the North, never to be heard from again. Theirs was a silent war against the elements instead of against the enemy.

Major Ed Crandall and Captain Bill McGilpin were two pilots who were lucky and they knew it. When forced down on the Greenland icecap in a C-47 loaded with passengers, they survived to tell of their experiences. Having flown to an isolated radar site to evacuate a frostbitten mechanic, they had landed safely, picked up the patient and were heading back to the Thule Air Base with an SA-16 Grumman *Albatross* flying cover for them. While on the ground they had had a fire in the right engine and therefore had requested the *Albatross* to watch them—just in case. Though they anticipated no trouble they felt better with the SA-16 near by, because it was equipped with floats and skis and could land either on water or on ice and snow.

Thirty minutes from Thule the left engine suddenly sputtered and died. Crandall feathered it and then increased power on the right engine. A few minutes later the overworked right engine began to lose power and the Gooney Bird began to sink toward the forbidding white desert below. Rather than take a chance on landing with two dead engines,

Crandall decided to make the landing immediately while he still had enough power to enable him to pick his landing spot.

Choosing a smooth plateau, he landed without difficulty as the SA-16 circled overhead. Two hours later the *Albatross* landed, took the scared, cold passengers of the C-47 aboard, and left for Thule. Major Crandall and his crew were left with the C-47 in the snow. The men packed blankets around the engines of the C-47 and waited, until about four hours later the Grumman returned and took them to Thule.

"Now here's where the story gets interesting," McGilpin said later. "The previous January the same type of incident had happened to another C-47. Although the plane was buried in the snow for three months, they managed to uncover it, change the engines under arduous circumstances and fly it out. We had visions of getting our C-47 out by the same means, but it didn't happen that way.

"The maintenance crews wanted nothing to do with changing engines on our plane with the temperature ranging from 40 to 60 degrees below zero, and to wait until the sun came up after the long winter would mean digging the airplane out from under tons of snow.

"What I say now I relate with bowed head—the Army had to pull us out of this one! They took one of their big caterpillar tractors and towed that sick Gooney Bird ninety miles back to Thule. Uphill, downhill, around treacherous crevasses, between nunataks, and down the side of the icecap; they towed her right into the hangar where she could be repaired. It seemed like that bent, broken old C-47 could always be patched up to go out and do a job that no other airplane could accomplish.

"One thing that has bothered me since, though, is how that Gooney Bird, strictly an Air Force airplane, must have felt when it had to be dragged out of that predicament by the Army."

On various occasions the C-47 flew without wing tips, with a fuselage and belly full of holes, with control cables broken, and even with much of its insides shot away. On occasion it flew when there was no visible means of support, like one day "down under" when it flew with only one wing. As far as can be determined, this was the only Gooney Bird ever to accomplish such a feat. The time was March 21, 1945, and the man riding in the copilot's seat at the time wasn't even a pilot. He was what pilots call a "ground pounder," and his name was Captain Jack Roberts, a communications specialist attached to the Army Airways Communications Service.

Although Roberts did not draw flying pay, he had a flying job that kept him in the air almost as much as the flight crews. He was an electronic communications expert who was required to assist in making periodic checks of low-frequency radio range facilities, the means by which a pilot could fly the beam and make instrument landings in bad weather. Auckland, New Zealand, had one of these installations and it had to be checked regularly.

Roberts always flew these missions in the copilot's seat of a C-47 *Dakota* with earphones clamped tightly to his head. As the pilot flew back and forth on the four invisible range legs, it was Roberts's job to listen carefully for "bends" and "fades"—conditions which might cause a fatal crash. Either one could lead a plane offcourse and into the sides of nearby mountains.

Jack had been doing this for months and he got a thrill from it, because the pilots would let him fly the plane from the copilot's seat to get "stick" time after the range-checking job was over for the day. He had wanted to go for pilot training but had not been able to qualify, and this was the only way he could get to fly.

Roberts and Flight Lieutenant Bade, a New Zealand Air Force pilot, took off from Whenuapai Airdrome near Auckland in midmorning for a two-hour range check. They crossed the radio range station at 1,300 feet to check the marker beacon receiver, but the light on the plane's instrument panel didn't register; so they made a 180-degree turn and climbed to 2,000 feet in order to make another pass over the station. It occurred to Roberts that the AACS radio mechanic might have forgotten to turn on the transmitter at the station below.

Since there was no way to contact the ground station transmitter, Roberts wanted to make doubly certain that the marker was not working. He asked Bade to fly out the northeast leg of the range to the fan marker site at Kaukapakapa, while still remaining at 2,000 feet.

They rode the right side of the beam leg, listening to the signal, and searched for the tiny white house that marked the transmitter site. Both men sat with their hands clasped to their headsets so they could clearly hear the signal and thus make certain they were flying in the center of the range leg. As they flew over the transmitter station, Roberts pointed to it. Bade nodded his head and then they both looked for the yellow light on the instrument panel but again it was not burning.

Roberts shrugged, looked at Bade, and was about to suggest that they return to Whenuapai, when out of the clouds slightly above them came a twin-engined Lockheed *Hudson* bomber, headed directly toward them. Before Bade could crank the wheel over and escape collision, the *Hudson* smashed into the left wing of the *Dakota*. The wing exploded into a thousand bits as the *Hudson* blasted through and disappeared. Bade wrestled with the controls trying to keep the airplane level. The rudder and elevator worked, but the ailerons proved useless. Bade now swung the aileron controls all the way to the right and added more power to the left engine, but nothing happened. He jammed in right rudder and skidded the airplane to compensate for the loss of the left wing. An airplane isn't supposed to fly with all the lift gone on one side, but this one did. Slowly, Bade was able to reverse his course and head back for the field.

Bade fought the *Dakota* all the way back to the base, and finally made a "controlled crash" on the end of the runway. When he cut the power on the left engine, the airplane veered violently to the left and staggered off the runway into the grass and then stopped. Bade cut the switches and, shaking, climbed out to inspect the damage.

The left wing had been sliced off almost up to the left engine cowling as if ripped by a giant knife. Wires and control cables dangled from the stub of what was left of the wing. Jagged metal hung down and gas from the wing tanks was spurting over the ground. With one glance, both men knew how closely they had come to disaster.

No one knows what kept the *Dakota* in the air. By all the principles of aerodynamics it should have spiraled steeply to the ground like a maple seed in the fall and as had the *Hudson* which, incidentally, killed its pilot. The Gooney Bird, however, had literally come in, as the old song goes, on a wing and a prayer.

No airplane engine will operate without gasoline and oil. This is a fact no pilot will deny. There are many grades of gasoline and oil, and engine manufacturers specify what is best for their products to gain maximum efficiency. But, like the aeronautical engineers who designed the venerable Gooney Bird, the Pratt and Whitney engine manufacturers who built the R-1830 engines powering it have been badly shaken by what some pilots have put in their gasoline and oil tanks. Automobile gasoline and extremely high-octane fuel have been used with ratings way below or above that specified by Pratt and Whitney. The grades of oil have varied from the type used in tractors to sewing machine oil, when all else was unavailable and a mission had to be flown. But the story that tops them all occurred in the South Pacific in 1944. Pratt and Whitney engineers don't believe it. Any C-47 pilot will.

It seems that a pilot was flying his C-47 into a forward air strip in New Guinea on a resupply mission. He was dozing in the left seat while the copilot flew the plane. Suddenly, the crew chief came forward, yelling, "Hey, Cap'n, we're losing oil out of the left engine!"

The young pilot jerked awake and looked out his window.

Flying into the forward airstrip where the enemy lurked was bad enough, but engine trouble in enemy territory was worse. Sure enough, oil was streaming out of the cowling, blowing small rivulets over the top of the wing.

"What's our position?" the captain yelled to his copilot.

"We've got about fifty miles to go," the copilot answered. "We ought to see land in a few minutes."

The radio operator, a youngster of seventeen, gripped the edge of his table. This was the first time in hundreds of hours in a C-47 that he had experienced an in-flight emergency, and he had wondered many times how it would feel. Should he break radio silence and send a distress call? He decided to wait for the pilot to tell him what to do.

The crew chief went back to the cabin and peered anxiously out the fuselage window. He had checked the life rafts stowed in the rear of the plane just in case they would have to be used.

The four men waited and wondered. They watched the ailing engine as the minutes dragged on. There is no way to tell how much oil is left in an oil tank from inside the plane. The only instrument is the oil pressure gauge and when the pressure dropped below operating pressure it would have to be shut down.

Suddenly the copilot shouted, "I see land! Beautiful land!"

The pilot took a final glance out his window at the leaky engine, then settled back in his seat. The plane couldn't let him down now, not after going this far. It never had. If all that oil hadn't caught fire by this time it probably never would, but even if the engine used all the oil they could still make it to the airfield without difficulty. They had a normal load and the other engine wasn't missing a beat.

They sighted the landing strip and the pilot brought the Gooney Bird in. The crew stepped out on the firm ground and inspected the streaks of black oil that splattered the wing and the engine cowling.

"Sarge, I'll bet you the price of a bottle that there isn't enough oil in that Maytag to oil your watch," the pilot said.

The sergeant found a stick, climbed up on the wing, and stuck it into the oil tank. "You're right, Captain. The stick isn't even damp."

"It looks like we've got a problem," the pilot said. "What do you think it is?"

"Nothing serious, sir. I can fix the leak," the sergeant assured him, "but what'll we do for oil?"

"You tell me, Sarge. You're the airplane doctor around here." The pilots went to the mess tent to grab a quick bite, while the two enlisted men stripped the cowling from the engine.

The airstrip, simply a rearmament strip with no aircraft operating from it, was used by C-47s to supply the infantry which was doing mop-up operations against the Japanese in the nearby hills. There were no maintenance facilities, no spare parts, no gasoline—and no oil.

The only personnel occupying the landing strip were armament specialists and a few supply men who controlled the issue of supplies as they were flown in. There were many shortages of supplies and a few huge overages. At mealtime it was everyone for himself to choose among the fruit cocktail, peanut butter, rice, crackers, and grapefruit juice, plus an odd assortment of dehydrated vegetables, Spam, and canned jelly. For some unknown reason, mountains of these food items and little else had piled up at the strip.

The tired crew lined up with the others to eat.

"Sorry I ain't got any gravy to put on this rice, Captain," the mess sergeant said, "but all I got is grape jelly. You might think that's queer, but it's all I got for the rice today. After you've been here as long as I have, you'll get used to it," he continued, his face expressionless.

The captain grimaced. Rice with grape jelly would be something to tell the kids about if he ever got home.

As the crew sat on up-ended boxes to eat, the sergeant stood near by and continued his apology. "I'm sorry we can't do better on food around here, but it's all I got. I got lots of grape jelly and gallons of Wesson oil. If you like cooking oil, I can get you plenty of that. That's all we had for the rice until the jelly showed up."

At those words the captain stiffened, dropped his GI fork in the rice and jelly mixture. "You say you got Wesson oil by the gallon?"

"Now wait a minute, Captain," interjected his copilot. "You're not thinking of . . .?"

"Hold it a minute. . . . Sarge, how much of that Wesson oil do you have?"

"Like I said, sir, I got gallons of it. Probably a hunnert." The sergeant looked at him quizzically. "Sir, you ain't goin' to put that stuff on the rice? It'll give you the runs. Now if you're looking for something to drink, I got a barrel of medical alco——"

"I don't want to eat or drink it, Sarge. I want it for my airplane!"

The mess sergeant, convinced that this pilot had gone loco, turned away muttering something like "rocks in the head," but the captain followed him.

"Look, Sarge, I'm not fooling. I want all the cooking oil you can spare."

"When we came out to fight this war, Captain, the Army figured they'd better buy enough of two things—cooking oil and grapefruit juice. They got all the grapefruit juice in Florida right here in this-here Pacific Ocean theater, and they got all the Wesson Oil in the world right on this-here island. What're you gonna use it for?"

"It's time you got an education, Sarge. You're going to see cooking oil used in a way you've never seen before and won't see again."

The rotund enlisted man blinked a couple of times and followed the captain to the jeep parked near by. At the edge of the jungle a soldier stood guard over the supply area. Searching through the maze of crates, they located one stack of boxes labeled "Wesson Oil."

Piling the back seat of the jeep high with the boxes, the captain and the sergeant roared back to the airplane. A few minutes later the empty oil tank was full of cooking oil. The crew scrambled aboard as the old sergeant stood shaking his head in disbelief.

The captain poked his head out of the left window of the C-47. "Hey, Sarge, thanks a lot. We got to get this crate into the blue before that thin oil drains out. See you again soon."

The sergeant stared openmouthed as the Gooney Bird taxied out and roared off toward the hills. "Judas!" he exclaimed. "The things you see in this part of the world when you ain't even had a drink!"

The Gooney Bird has flown an infinite variety of cargoes in its day. You name it and if it will fit inside the fuselage, chances are it has been flown from one point to another in the C-47. During World War II, some cargo was even flown on the outside of the airplane, as witness the time in the South Pacific when P-40 and B-25 wings were strapped underneath the fuselage and flown to forward airstrips.

Passengers, however, have never flown on the outside of the airplane—that is, paying passengers. But there was the time when a hitchhiker rode outside and thus set another "first" for the incomparable Gooney Bird.

October 9, 1950, was a night Captain Jorge L. Guzman, a pilot for LAMSA Airlines in Mexico, will never forget. The run from Torreón to Mexico City was supposed to be routine. The weather was clear and cold, and he carried half a planeload of passengers, some cargo and a little mail—about the usual load for his DC-3.

Captain Guzman taxied into run-up position on the Torreon runway, checked his engines and lined up for take-off. He gave it the throttles and watched the runway lights slip by as the DC-3 slowly picked up speed. But something didn't feel right. He had flown this particular airplane many times, but this time the tail seemed heavier than usual and the airplane didn't accelerate as quickly as it usually did.

Finally, after what seemed a long time to Guzman, the tail lifted and the main landing gear came off the ground. The copilot pulled up the landing gear and as soon as he did both pilots noticed a slight vibration they had never noticed before, the kind of vibration sometimes caused when tires are worn and spin unevenly in the wheel wells.

Guzman applied the brakes to the spinning wheels but the vibration continued. He asked the copilot to check the cowl flaps, thinking he had forgotten to close them when the plane took off, but the flaps were in the "trail" position excactly where they should have been. Guzman shrugged his shoulders and watched the instruments in the dimly lighted cockpit, while the copilot reduced the power settings for the long night climbout. Then the vibration suddenly ceased and they temporarily forgot about it.

The climbout from Torreón at night is tricky. The safest way is to follow the radio range just as in instrument conditions, but this procedure to Captain Guzman was "old hat." He had flown the route many times. He leveled off at 12,000 feet and settled down for the long flight to Mexico City, as the passengers settled comfortably in their seats for the three-and-one-half-hour nap they expected to get.

Guzman went through the usual procedure of reducing the power on both engines, closing the cowl flaps, and trimming the airplane for level flight. When he had done this the vibration returned. The controls shook back and forth with a chattering motion, and the rudder pedals fluttered. Guzman looked at the instruments, but each one showed that the airplane, for all practical purposes, was functioning normally. He looked at the engines, but they didn't seem to be vibrating. Puzzled, he continued on course for another ten minutes trying to make up his mind what the trouble was. If it weren't the cowl flaps or the engines, what could it be? Were the wing flaps partially down? He checked them. No, they were up. Could it be that one propeller wasn't balanced? He couldn't check that from the cockpit, except perhaps from engine vibration. Perhaps the door was open? No, it was closed.

He had to make up his mind what to do. He had passengers to consider and his decision had to be in favor of safety. It was night and if he had to make a forced landing in the mountains he could expect nothing but disaster. He decided to return to Torreón.

Guzman advised the control tower at Torreón of his decision and he was cleared immediately for his long descent and approach to the field. Several minutes later his wheels touched the runway. He held a little more power than usual on the final approach but as soon as he flared out, the airplane quit flying completely and the tail clumped down with a shuddering thud. That was unusual. The tail of a DC-3 doesn't usually settle that quickly unless the pilot deliberately makes a three-point landing, and Captain Guzman hadn't attempted that. He had tried to make a normal wheels-first landing.

He wasted no time taxiing to the ramp. As soon as he braked to a stop he unhooked his safety belt, grabbed his flashlight and went out the cabin door. He told his passengers to keep their seats while he made a quick check with his ground crew.

When he turned his flashlight on the tail surfaces of the DC-3 he saw something he could hardly believe. A human form was draped over the left horizontal stabilizer.

"*Que pasa, hombre?*" he called. "Get down off there."

The figure didn't move. Guzman went closer to shine his light in the eyes of the stranger. It was a young boy about sixteen years old. His shirt had been completely ripped off and he was frozen so stiff he could hardly move.

Captain Guzman reached up and dragged the boy off the horizontal stabilizer, and after a few minutes the lad was able to talk. He had flown for fifty-seven minutes on Guzman's DC-3 by clinging to the leading edge of the tail surface by his armpits!

When he was thawed out enough to be able to give a coherent story, the boy told the pilot that he was a farm boy named Cliserio Reyes Guerrero and that he had wanted nothing more than a free ride to Mexico City. He didn't get to his destination, but he had become the first—and last—human being ever to ride on the outside of a DC-3 in flight.

Cliserio Reyes Guerrero was impressed with his first flight and had no intention of letting it be his last one. He later took flight training and became a pilot in the Mexican Air Force.

Five for
the Hall
of Fame

7

The first daylight jump of the 101st Airborne Division took place on September 17, 1944, a little more than two months after the Normandy landing. We in the Division called it a "Parade Ground" jump because of its perfection. It was the best that the division had ever made in combat or in training. Much of the credit for the success of the operation has to go to that old workhorse, the C-47. Only three of the 428 planes involved failed to reach the drop zones. Generally, the story was the same for the plane throughout all campaigns. The troopers liked it and the men who flew it.

—General Maxwell D. Taylor

More than 10,000 Douglas DC-2s and DC-3s have squatted on the world's flight lines in the last three decades. It would be impossible to compile a total of the flying hours attributed to the entire fleet of Gooney Birds; however, we can assume that each airplane that flew for a few years had thousands of hours under its wings. We can also assume that each airplane took its crew through at least one hair-raising experience. The authors found literally thousands of such cases in their research for this book—all of which proved time and again how indomitable is the plane that Douglas wrought. Five of these stories are repeated here as representative of the reasons why the Gooney Bird will forever have a place in the aeronautical Hall of Fame.

Until the Japanese captured Rangoon in 1942, one merchant had been fabulously rich and well respected. Now he was just one among the hundreds of refugees that surrounded the DC-2s and DC-3s at the Burmese jungle airstrip, seeking passage out of the path of the rampaging Japanese Army. Every man, woman, and child there was ready to storm the planes to get inside if the guards relaxed their watch. Terror was in their eyes as they pushed and shoved. Their hands held out pleadingly.

"I'll pay you twenty thousand pounds," the merchant whispered to the China National Aviation Corporation (CNAC) Operations manager who was calmly packing twice as many passengers into each plane as it was designed to hold. "Twenty thousand pounds sterling for passage to India," the man repeated softly so as not to be overheard.

The manager didn't even look at the man as he said, "You will have to wait your turn. All the money in the world won't buy you a seat out of turn."

The man stayed, hounding and begging each time a DC-3 was readied for take-off. He became a nuisance but his money was worthless; he never did get passage.

That's the way it was on every transport that flew refugees out of Burma in 1942. Terrified people were willing to pay fantastic prices and give up all their worldly possessions for passage to safety. The CNAC pilots, had they been greedy, could have made fortunes in a few days. To their eternal credit, they were more interested in saving lives than in making money.

For more than a month the steady stream of refugees had

been moving northward over the treacherous route to India. Airplanes could evacuate only a small fraction of the total, so thousands took to the mountain trails. How many lived through the trek, how many made it across to safety, how many died and were left behind, is unknown. The great majority of them were Indian and Burmese, but some were American and British. Many came from as far away as Rangoon, escaping first to Mandalay, then to Lashio, just one step ahead of the Japanese. Every motor vehicle that could move was jammed with humanity. Overhead the sharp-nosed fighters of General Claire Chennault's Flying Tigers cruised, looking for harassing Japanese *Zeros* bent on strafing the endless column of humanity. At concentration points deep in the jungles the refugees hid during the daytime, and then, at dusk, some of them, the lucky ones, were loaded into the Gooneys and whisked off to safety.

The evacuation of refugees from the British crown colony of Hong Kong off the southeast coast of China was different. Escape could only be made by air or sea. Air escape meant sneaking the DCs through Japanese-controlled skies and into the international airport. The airfield at Hong Kong had never been an ideal base due to the hazardous approaches near the mountains. After the terrible beating it had taken from Japanese bombings, there remained only one narrow strip that could be used as a runway. Even this runway was pitted with three bomb holes and bordered by the smoking wreckage of several ruined transports which had been caught on the ground. The only field lights were three red kerosene lanterns which were placed on the edge of the bomb craters to mark their positions. There were landing lights on the field, but they were switched on only when a plane was ready for immediate take-off and extinguished as soon as the plane was airborne.

Because they wished to avoid bringing further excitement to the battle-weary population, the pilots would take off at fifteen-minute intervals, swing down the channel toward the Japanese lines, then turn northward toward their objective of

Namyung 175 miles away. If they could, they would return for a second trip before dawn. Two of the planes on one particular night were able to return and evacuated a total of 276 refugees.

Veteran CNAC pilot, Captain Harold Sweet, however, was not so fortunate. When the Japs first attacked Hong Kong his plane had been in the hangar waiting to have the left engine changed because it had developed a bad main bearing. When he took off a few days before the city capitulated, he did so with a prayer on his lips, a prayer that the old engine, which had been hastily reassembled, would continue to operate long enough for him to get his load of frightened people to safety.

Just as he crossed the border into Free China, the left engine spluttered, backfired and died. Sweet looked down upon the blackened countryside hoping to see a place where he could set the Douglas down. The remaining engine wouldn't keep the plane in the air with the load he had. He picked out a tiny postage stamp of a field that seemed level and landed. As soon as it stopped rolling, the plane sank hub deep into sticky mud. Fifty-four passengers piled out of Sweet's DC-3 and stood behind the wings and tail and shoved as Sweet gunned the good engine in an effort to dislodge the plane from the mud. In spite of their best efforts, the airplane remained stuck all night.

At dawn of the next day, Sweet and his passengers gathered leaves, tree branches, and tall grass to camouflage the plane from the searching eyes of Japanese fighter pilots. Just as the job was finished and they felt certain the airplane was well hidden, five Mitsui fighters streaked in low and opened up with small-caliber machine guns. Sweet and his charges scattered for cover and watched helplessly as the enemy planes flew back and forth over the transport, blasting it until their ammunition was exhausted.

Sweet had used excellent foresight when he landed and had drained the oil and gasoline out of the plane so it wouldn't catch fire if strafed on the ground. When the Japs were gone, Sweet and his passengers crawled from hiding to look at the damage. The propellers, tires, wings, instruments, and fuselage were riddled so that it looked like a giant sieve. Sweet counted more than 3,000 bullet holes in the wings and fuselage alone!

In spite of the holes, Sweet found that none of the main structural members were severely damaged. If parts were available and could be brought in, the old bird might, just might, fly again. Too many people depended upon the airplane for their lives, in some way it would have to be repaired.

Sweet hiked to a nearby village where he found a wireless set and contacted Chungking radio. He got in touch with Ted Soldinski, CNAC's maintenance wizard, a man who could breathe life into an airplane if anyone could. Soldinski arrived that same day with tools and spare parts, studied the damage and immediately set to work on the engines and instruments, while the coolies patched the bullet holes with canvas and home-made glue. Tires were replaced and the tanks were filled with oil and gas.

When Soldinski finally pronounced the plane flyable, it was Charles Sharp, Operations manager for CNAC, who undertook to fly it on to India where it could be put in better shape.

The engines ran extremely rough and spat such streaks of flame out the exhausts that the whole plane seemed to be on fire. Shortly after take-off a rudder control cable snapped, making it difficult to control the plane. It yawed and wallowed, but Sharp managed to keep it upright by use of the ailerons. He knew he might have difficulty landing with the broken cable, but at least he would be in free country. He flew straight ahead into the face of a 30-mile-per-hour wind. To save the engines, he throttled back until he was flying on the ragged edge of a stall. The propellers seemed to be barely turning as he pulled the pitch control back to 1650 rpm.

Somehow, and Sharp could never explain how, it took him only 8 hours and 12 minutes to cover the 904 miles to his first objective. He landed without difficulty, despite the broken cable, loaded on seven more refugees whose pleas he could not ignore, and headed the fire-spitting plane back into the night clouds. This time his route took him over the Japanese lines. Controlling the plane was still difficult, but the clouds were his protection and he needed all he could find.

Once inside the clouds, tropical rains battered the plane like sprays of bullets, but above the staccato was the reassuring throb of the engines. Suddenly a shrill, piercing whistling note broke through the synchronized drone of the engines. The whistling sound became almost deafening. Sharp knew the answer—the rain was washing off the canvas patches that had been stuck on with the coolies' home-made glue!

The weird cacophony of shrill whistles increased in tone and pitch until it reached an agonizing crescendo just as the plane broke out into the clear—headlong into a patrol of six Japanese fighter planes going in the opposite direction. The Japanese passed so close that Sharp and his passengers could clearly see the orange fireball markings on their planes.

The Japs, recognizing the familiar shape of the unarmed transport, turned and streaked back toward it. As they closed in for the kill, they were startled by the shrieking of the air through the hundreds of holes in the transport's skin. Without firing a shot, the enemy fighters suddenly broke away and disappeared into the clouds, leaving the DC-3 unmolested.

Two hours later a tired, shaken Charles Sharp approached his destination airfield in India and landed. An Army major met the airplane and exclaimed, "Whistling Willie! Why did you bother to radio us? We've heard you for the past fifty miles!"

It was then that Sharp realized that the bullet holes had probably saved his life. The airplane had set up such an eerie wail that it had actually scared the Japanese away.

Maybe the Japs were out of gasoline for the next three days and night; but whatever happened, no CNAC planes were threatened by anything more serious than weather.

"Whistling Willie" became the subject of a cryptic Tokyo broadcast: "Enemy forces are moving into northern Burma in force. [Actually, there wasn't a handful of American soldiers within 400 miles.] Spearhead of their invasion is a new aerial weapon, designed foolishly to unnerve the Emperor's pilots who hold mastery of the Burma skies. This secret weapon spouts streams of flame and screeches in horrible tones as it flies. The white man's folly will forthwith be driven from the Asiatic Heavens!"

As an aftermath to "Whistling Willie's" experience, Chinese spies in Namyung relayed reports of bewildered Japanese pilots who had searched desperately for the CNAC transport that Tojo had given them credit for destroying. Could it be that the Japanese pilots who had seen the flame-belching airplane and had run away from it were the same ones who had strafed it? They had thoroughly pelted it with bullets on the ground, yet there it was, flying along as serenely as ever, like an apparition, a ghost. Luckily for Sharp and his load of people, the Japanese were superstitious.

The saga of "Whistling Willie," flying while full of bullet holes, is difficult to top, yet this was only one of many incidents concerning the planes and pilots of the China National Aviation Corporation. Another incident, and just as fantastic, concerns the DC-3 that flew with a borrowed wing built for its sister ship, the smaller DC-2. After its "operation" and test flight, it was named the DC-2½.

On a regularly scheduled passenger flight from Hong Kong to Chungking, one of the six DC-3s operated by the "Middle Kingdom Space Machine Family," as the Chinese called the CNAC, was forced down at Suifu because of a Japanese air raid on Hong Kong.

The Japanese bombers, having completed their destruction, were headed home when one of the pilots spotted the DC-3 on the ground at Suifu. Five bombers pounced upon the transport, sending the grounded passengers and crew scurrying for cover. The Japs dropped more than two hundred bombs on the airfield, and when they left the area CNAC Captain H. L. Woods came out to look at the mess.

One bomb had passed through the right wing of the aircraft and exploded underneath. The explosion had torn off the wing just outside the point where it joined the center section. The fuselage, ripped horribly, was marked by about fifty shrapnel holes. The concussion had knocked the airplane sideways for more than six feet, but the gasoline tanks had not exploded. Fortunately, other than a ruined wing and the holes in the fuselage, there was no serious damage to the engines or to other vital parts.

Woods's solution to the problem was plain and simple—the plane needed a new wing. He knew, however, that there was none in Hong Kong to fit the DC-3. Perhaps someone in Hong Kong could locate one for him, although getting it to Suifu would be a problem. Suifu is located about 900 miles in the interior of China, and the only surface means of transportation from Hong Kong was over the Burma Road, which might mean a wait of several months, if they could get the wing to him there at all. The enforced idleness of one plane for that long would be a bitter blow to the Chinese and there was always the risk that the Japanese would return and destroy the airplane.

Woods rounded up several hundred coolies. They dragged the crippled plane off the shell-marked field and three miles down the road to hide it in the dense bamboo. Camouflaging it as best they could, they waited. As had been feared, the Japanese returned, and for three days fifty-seven bombers pounded the airfield and the town of Suifu. The bamboo fooled the attackers, however, and not a hit was scored on the DC-3

Captain Woods radioed Hong Kong and asked the company's representative there to try and locate a DC-3 wing. A short time later Hong Kong wired Woods: "Sending DC-2 wing. Try it."

The job of getting the DC-2 wing to Suifu was a major aviation feat in itself. It was impossible to get the wing inside another airplane, so something else had to be tried. Someone suggested that it be bolted to the bottom of the airplane, under the belly, and carried across the mountains to Suifu. This idea, while seeming sound, posed an aerodynamic as well as a weight-and-balance problem. The maintenance men finally decided it was worth a try, but that it should be done butt end forward for the best weight distribution.

Two inspection covers were removed from the DC-2 wing's butt end and guy wires were attached. The same was done at the wing tip. Then holes were drilled through the floor of the DC-3 and the wires threaded through and made fast inside the fuselage. The wing was guyed fore, aft, and sideways. Plywood fairings were fashioned around the butt for streamlining.

Captain Harold Sweet, of "Whistling Willie" fame, said he would fly the wing to Suifu, if the airplane would get off the ground. Since it hadn't been done before, Sweet and the others were a little skeptical. But it was rough in China and men often had to live by taking chances.

Sweet raised the DC-3 into the sky, and the load didn't seem to bother the flight characteristics of the plane. He climbed slowly, flying in wide circles to keep out of range of the Jap gunners spotted around the city and harbor of Hong Kong. Little by little the plane gained altitude; he circled again and headed for Suifu. Except for a slight buffeting and a longitudinal instability, Sweet found that the DC-3 flew without difficulty. After an uneventful trip, he set down at the shell-torn field at Suifu and supervised the unbolting of the spare wing.

The DC-2 was an eleven-passenger airplane designed to lift a maximum weight of 18,600 pounds, and with a wingspan of eighty-five feet. The DC-3, a twenty-one passenger plane weighing a maximum of 24,400 pounds, had a wingspan of ninety-five feet. The DC-2 wing was, therefore, five feet shorter. Fortunately, the butt ends of the wings were identical and could be bolted on interchangeably, but there the similarity ended. The DC-2 wing was designed to carry about three-fourths of the gross weight of a DC-3. Supposedly, then, it would be impossible to fly a DC-3 with one DC-2 and one DC-3 wing. The shape, area and taper of the two wings are entirely different.

The whole story of aviation's progress is one of conquest over seemingly insurmountable obstacles. Men have been injured and killed because of trying innovations designed to perfect the flying characteristics of airplanes, but for every accident or death in the probing and experimenting there have come new ideas to further aviation.

The DC-2½, as it was now called, was flown back to Hong Kong by veteran pilot Harold Sweet. He had surprisingly little trouble. The DC-2½ had a tendency to roll toward the shorter wing but he corrected this by setting his aileron trim tab twelve degrees to the opposite side. With this adjustment, and with a slight difference in the propeller settings, the airplane flew the 900 miles back home straight and level.

There doesn't seem to be any limit to the capability of the airplane that Douglas built. In the steaming jungles, where corrosion caused considerable damage to metal, rubber, and fabric, the C-47 stood up well. Even when ditched in the ocean, it has been surfaced and reconditioned and put back into service.

One of the most unusual stories about stamina and ability to withstand extremes comes from Iceland, where a Gooney Bird tangled with Vatna Jokull Glacier, known as "the world's deadliest glacier." This plane, Serial Number 1013, belonged to the USAF Air Rescue Service and had been on many rescue missions in the past. This, story, however, concerns an incident in which the C-47 itself had to be saved. The man most familiar with the story is Lieutenant Colonel Perry C. Emmons, an officer who was assigned as Mission Commander responsible for recovering the airplane if he could:

"I was on temporary duty in Keflavík in 1950," Colonel Emmons recalls, "shortly after an Icelandic Airlines DC-4 was reported missing. I received a message from the commander of Air Rescue Service putting me in charge of rescue operations.

"Our Air Rescue plane searched for three days and finally located the DC-4 on top of Vatna Jokull Glacier in the northeastern part of the island. One rescue plane made contact with the downed crew and learned that everyone was alive and well. They also learned that snow conditions on the glacier were ideal for ski-plane operation.

"I contacted the rescue unit at Bluie West One, Greenland, and asked them to send a ski-equipped C-47 to the crash scene immediately. A short time later Number 1013 arrived at Keflavík.

"The C-47, equipped with four JATO (jet-assisted take-off) bottles, took off for Vatna Jokull to recover the stranded people. The weather was excellent and I thought it would be a routine mission.

"I was in the control tower at Keflavík, in contact with Number 1013 as it winged toward the crash site, and I talked to the pilot as he made his ski landing on the snow. Everything was perfect for the pickup. The plane took on the stranded survivors. All that remained was to take off and fly to Keflavík. But it didn't work out that way.

"The Gooney Bird pilot goosed the throttles but the plane didn't budge. He tried again and again, jazzing the throttles, but the bird was stuck solid. When the metal skis touched the snow on landing the friction had warmed them just enough to slightly melt the snow beneath. Then it had immediately refrozen, welding the plane tightly. The pilot rocked the plane with the throttles, but to no avail; finally he told the crew chief to get out and rock the wings to unstick the skis, to break them from the ice.

"Finally the pilot decided to fire two JATO bottles. While the crew chief rocked the wings the pilot flicked the switches cutting loose the blast of air from the cylinders beneath the plane. The Gooney broke loose under full power and moved forward while the crew chief waved and yelled for the plane to stop and pick him up. About that time it dawned on the pilot that the crew chief was stranded, so he circled back for him.

"Loading the sergeant aboard, he gunned the engines, but the thing was stuck again! However, the pilot was sharp this time. He punched the JATO button, thus firing the last two bottles. The plane broke loose and inched slowly over the ice and snow; so slowly, in fact, that it wouldn't fly!

"With all four JATO bottles gone, there was nothing left to do but stop the engines and think. He could radio for more JATOs. If two wouldn't get him off, perhaps four would if used all at once.

"Well, I sent messages to Greenland requesting JATO bottles but got no immediate response. After the rescue airplane got stuck, an Icelandic ground party fought its way to the treacherous top of the glacier and to the stranded C-47. The leader of the party told the pilot that it would be unwise for the crew to remain with the airplane longer than a few hours because he believed bad weather was about to set in. The pilot and crew decided to leave with the ground party and let the Gooney Bird face the weather alone. Even if JATO bottles could be located it might take several days to fly them in.

"So old Number 1013 was left stranded on the glacier—one lone C-47 against the elements of Vatna Jokull. But this is not, by any means, the end of the story. This Gooney, suffice it to say, simply went into a long period of hibernation.

"I was certain in my own mind that the Gooney could be flown off the glacier, but I wasn't sure of how to go about it. I intended to find out.

"Eight days later I radioed Air Rescue Service Headquarters with a plan for recovering the bird. I told my commander that I wanted approval to get together a qualified group of men and to leave soon as possible. I would be the mission commander and I would need a C-47 pilot with

C-47 ski-wheel experience, a good copilot and two top-notch maintenance men. Also, I wanted to take along a pararescue team to be on standby at Keflavík in case we needed them for medical aid.

"The boss bought my idea one hundred per cent. We assembled the recovery party and all the necessary equipment at Keflavík around the middle of October, which was almost a month from the time the bird got stranded. But on the day following the party's arrival in Iceland, I made a flight over Vatna Jokull to look the site over. I wanted to know if everything was as the crew had left it. There old Number 1013 sat, cold, forlorn and helpless. The weather had changed very little and the snow had not covered it much during the previous month.

It looked to me as if we could do the job, but at this time a series of uncontrollable delays occurred, which were to spell defeat for the project. I couldn't help squirming at the nature of the delays because at any time bad weather might set in and I felt there would be no getting that Gooney out of Iceland.

"Finally we ironed things out. The recovery party left Keflavík and got to Vatna Jokull on November 2nd. As I had feared, however, the weather changed and snow fell heavily. For the next two weeks the glacier was completely closed in by weather. We couldn't even fly over to check on the Gooney.

"On November 14th the weather cleared enough for me to take an airplane and go take a look. When I found the plane it lay buried in the snow with only the tip of its rudder showing above the white blanket. That did it. We canceled all our plans for recovery and abandoned the project.

"The following spring an Icelandic ground party decided to have a look at the Gooney. Kris Oleson and Alfred Eliasson, owners and operators of Icelandic Airlines—now minus its DC-4—were close to bankruptcy and wanted that abandoned C-47. They took along a bulldozer, and when they found the plane they set to work uncovering it. They cleaned the snow out and dragged the plane down to the edge of the glacier. The weight of the snow had collapsed the landing gear, but this didn't bother Oleson and Eliasson too much. They jacked the old bird up and tied some two-by-fours to the gear so it wouldn't collapse again. Oleson got into the cockpit and began playing around with the switches. By all rights, the batteries, after having been buried in the snow for more than eight months, shouldn't have been any good. But Oleson was experienced enough of the Far North to know that the Arctic worked strange miracles. Perhaps this was one of them. He flipped one of the starter switches and the engine turned over briefly. (I know what took place because I was flying overhead at the time, watching what was happening.) After a few minutes' wait, Oleson hit the starter switch again. This time the engine started and smoke belched out in huge puffs. I expected the engine to blow up, but it kept on running. Oleson must have been smiling down there in that frozen airplane, and to continue his enjoyment he started the other engine.

"I could hardly believe what I saw—that any airplane, after being buried for months in the snow, would start and run smoothly. It seemed to be running as good as the one I was flying overhead!

"Oleson's party kicked a few boulders out of the way and bulldozed a take-off strip. They climbed aboard like they were at a busy air terminal and Oleson poured on the coal. The snow flew in great clouds. The old bird shifted uneasily on the snow, settled into a straightforward motion, bounced off the rough, crude strip, and reached for the sky."

The gamble that Kris Oleson and Al Eliasson and their financial backers had taken to acquire the abandoned C-47 paid off. They had offered the United States Air Force $700 for the airplane and the offer had been accepted. This sum, plus the cost of renting the tractors and pay for the ground party—a total of about $5,000—bought them an airplane to replace their lost DC-4. The DC-3 was flown to England for modification but even before work began, a Spanish airline offered Oleson $80,000 for it. The offer was promptly accepted. The $75,000 profit enabled them to make a down payment on a DC-6. Today, Icelandic Airlines plies the northern route between New York and Europe and is solvent. Thanks to the fabulous durability and indestructibility of the airplane that can do the seemingly impossible.

C-47s, like any other machinery, are only as good as the maintenance and care given them by the men who use or fly them. Compare them to automobiles or other equipment. The man who takes care of his machine is the one who will realize the greatest use from it. Airplanes during World War II were put to grueling tests. Pilots who flew them either loved them or abused them. At the same time the airplane was performing, so were the crews being put to rigid tests to see how long they could withstand the rigors of war. Such a man was Lieutenant George Walker, just another pilot on the roster in New Guinea. His airplane, just another Gooney Bird, was christened "The Long Island Duck."

George Walker, a racing car driver, had made the circuits all over the United States and South America. Just prior to Pearl Harbor he had had an accident which kept him grounded until after the war was in full swing. He worked in a defense plant making precision instruments, but the lure of adventure was too great for him to sit out the war in a factory. He thought he might be able to beat the age deadline and enter flying cadet training, and when he announced to his wife that he intended to learn to fly her only comment was, "Now, at least, you'll have the whole United States Army looking out for you."

Walker passed the physical, passed all phases of flying school satisfactorily, and was assigned to a C-47 unit for transition training at Austin, Texas. To Walker this was highly disappointing because he had his heart set on flying fighter planes. From the start George Walker hated the C-47, not realizing that one day he would grow to love the old bird. He grumbled secretly to himself, but tried never to let his disgust show to others.

When the transition phase was completed, Walker was assigned to a Troop Carrier Group in which he towed gliders and trained with paratroopers until he was pronounced qualified for combat duty.

Cabin tanks were installed in his plane at Fort Wayne, Indiana. From there he flew to Hamilton Field, California, the overseas jumping-off point. One night, shortly after dark, he took off, passed over the Golden Gate Bridge and 15 hours later landed in Hawaii. From there his route was to Christmas Island, Samoa, Fiji, New Caledonia, and finally Townsville, Australia. There his long-range gas tanks were removed and he shoved off for Port Moresby, New Guinea. Here he began the battle with the flies, the mosquitoes, and the heat.

During his first two months in New Guinea he flew all manner of cargo in formation with other transport pilots in order to learn the ropes. Most of these cargo missions were heavily escorted by fighter airplanes, and Walker's role thus far was certainly not unique.

Less than a month after his arrival in New Guinea he had his first hardship, even though he had not yet seen the enemy. On one of the formation flights, Walker's copilot, Lieutenant Howard Zimmerman, was flying the airplane while Walker dozed. Suddenly there was a horrible crash and the airplane rocked and wallowed wildly in the sky. It nosed up and threatened to stall, and the two men fought to bring it under control. It took them only seconds to realize that another airplane had rammed their plane.

When Walker saw the turned-up wing tip and splintered metal whipping in the slipstream, he knew he had been hit hard and had to set the plane down in a hurry. In the distance he saw a stream bed that he might be able to reach, but quickly dispensed with that idea when the plane began to buffet violently. He had to get down quickly, before he lost control.

"Bail out!" Walker yelled, knowing the airplane was eventually going to crash.

Lieutenant Seymour Rosenfield, the navigator, ran to the

rear of the airplane to get parachutes for the crew. He returned quickly, his face ashen.

"George," he said shakingly, "there are only four chutes. There are five of us."

Walker mulled over Rosenfield's words. Finally he said, "You fellows bail out. I'll set this bird down in the swamp. Now get going!"

No one moved. The other crew members stared at him. Finally Zimmerman said, "We're staying, George."

That was that. Five men—four parachutes. None of them would be used.

Sergeant Braden, the engineer, had been injured in the midair collision. When the two planes had collided, Braden, standing in the cabin, had been thrown against the side of the fuselage, wrenching his back severely.

At the last crucial moment Walker saw a small clearing and headed for it. The crippled Gooney was steadily losing altitude and he knew he was, at best, going to make what pilots call "a controlled crash."

Walker's judgment was good and he made a perfect approach—not too high and not too low. As he leveled off he felt the tall marsh grass scrape the belly of the plane. Zimmerman cut the switches to prevent the plane from catching fire on impact. Walker heaved the wheel back into his stomach, holding the nose high and forcing the tail down. The C-47 squashed into the soft ooze, slid forward for a short distance and stopped, with a prolonged sucking sound as it settled into the slosh. It was all over—all but the long trek out.

While they pondered what to do, a C-47 from Walker's squadron flew over them. Walker and his crew waved to indicate that they were down safely. Later that evening other C-47s flew over and dropped packages of food, water, and medicine, many of which fell into the swamp and were lost.

That night the crew slept in the airplane and battled the ever-present mosquitoes. Several days then passed and no more planes appeared. Walker wondered if they had been forgotten and if they would have to find their own way out. Six days after the crash, a rescue party arrived, and on the morning of the seventh day they left the crumpled wreckage of the Gooney Bird and trekked laboriously out of the swamp and onto more solid ground. One man in the ground rescue party had stepped on a rusty nail in a packing crate, his wound had festered, and, unable to walk, he had to be carried, as did Sergeant Braden whose wrenched back was causing him great pain.

That afternoon they reached the village of Popo on the Kapouri River, where they washed, ate, and relaxed. On the eighth day they paddled down the river to its mouth; then walked a short distance to the Lalappi River, where they boarded a river launch. Late that evening they reached Terapo, which had been a trading post before the war. There they found a small radio transmitter and were able to contact their home base. The following day a C-47 landed and picked them up, just ten days after they had crashed.

Walker described his tour of duty from that point on and showed what was asked of the C-47 in that theater of war:

"For the next several months our work was moving and supplying the Australian forces as they fought their way up the valley from Nadzab to Kaipit, Gusap, and Dumpu on the southern end of New Guinea; supplying outposts in the surrounding mountains, and dropping supplies to places with names like Shaggy Ridge. We ate dehydrated eggs, Spam, and bully beef. We flew from dawn to dusk and piled up lots of flying time, most of which was without fighter cover. We hopped from target to target almost at treetop level to evade Japanese pilots, and our landing fields were rough and dirty and much too short for safety.

"One day I was flying a group of Aussie infantrymen back from Dumpu to Nadzab. Near the airstrip I received landing instructions, and as I put my wheels down I glanced out my window just in time to see an explosion on the ground. I wondered what they were blasting. At that moment I saw a B-25 bomber explode, and I knew that I had lumbered in right into the middle of an enemy air raid. Several Japanese *Zeros* were strafing the airfield, some buildings were on fire, and when a couple of Jap fighters turned in my direction I knew my bird would be a sitting duck.

"Without waiting to see more, I yanked up the flaps on my C-47 and yelled to the copilot to jerk up the landing gear. With the *Zeros* in sight, I dove for a small, winding stream, part of the Ramu River, which led to Lae. Trees lined both banks. I dropped the C-47 down until I was flying between the trees, trying to keep my wing tips from hitting them. The *Zeros* either hadn't seen us or had lost us in the confusion as we snaked our way at treetop level over the narrow river. I went on to Lae and landed. Several of my Aussie passengers got out and actually kissed the ground. These hard-bitten veterans had seen the roughest kind of war, but they had been just as scared as I was.

"Several days later, when we were taking off from Gusap, I blew a tire. Since I was already committed for take-off, I jerked the bird off the ground and staggered into the air. When I reached Nadzab, the tower operator advised me to come in for a belly landing. I thought about it for a while and decided that since we were already short on airplanes, I wasn't about to wreck this one. Luckily we had a good strong head wind to burn up our fuel and the airplane was almost empty. I was able to bring it in on one wheel and control the direction with the throttles and brakes with no damage at all. It wasn't a question of my superior flying ability, but rather a tribute to the remarkable flying characteristics of the C-47.

"I had been looking forward to a leave in Australia, but since I had grown accustomed to disappointments thus far in my service I wasn't at all surprised to learn that I had been scheduled for three days' temporary duty to Aitape.

"Assigned to me as copilot was Lieutenant 'Slim' Moore, Sergeant Helm was my crew chief, and Sergeant Gomeringer was my radio operator. My airplane, named by Major Donald

Woods who lived near me on Long Island in New York, was named 'The Long Island Duck.'

"One morning just after sunrise we took off, flew up the valley, bypassed the Japanese stronghold at Wewak and landed at Aitape. All Troop Carrier pilots had been ordered to avoid Wewak because of reports that an estimated 50,000 Japanese had been cut off and trapped there. One of our C-47s had dive-bombed and strafed Wewak one day with hand grenades and a tommy gun, and they vouched for the fact that the Japs were there. Aitape had been taken in April of 1944 and had since served as a bulwark between Wewak and Hollandia. Our job was to work with and supply the units of the 32nd Infantry Division, which was having one devil of a rough time fighting its way in.

"The Aitape airstrip ran parallel to, and was only a short distance from, the beach. The surrounding terrain was thick jungle extending back several miles to steep-faced mountains. The Intelligence officer briefed us and flew with us on the first mission to point out the dropping areas—three of which were cinches, but the other looked as if it would be impossible to drop supplies anywhere near the drop zone.

"As luck would have it, the toughest drop site was also the most important. It was at an advanced position approximately fifteen to twenty miles southeast of Aitape airstrip. An extremely small clearing, not more than a mile from the foot of the mountain, it was located on the north side of a hill several hundred yards back from a wide, dry river bed which extended from the mountains to the beach.

"The best pattern for this drop was to fly east along the foot of the mountains, approach the river bed, bank sharply to the left around the hill and slow the airplane by dropping partial flaps. The next step was to aim the airplane at a spot which looked greener than the rest of the jungle—the drop area.

"I pretended that I was landing the airplane and would get the old bird to shiver almost at the point of stalling right

over the target, because the drop area was so small and so
difficult to hit that this was the only way to make an accurate drop. The men on the ground needed those supplies,
and if they were dropped even a few feet into the jungle the
troops would never be able to get to them.

To regain flying speed after almost stalling over the target,
I would dive down to the river bed at my right, while
keeping away from the east side of the river where the Japs
were waiting for me with small-arms fire. Along the river
bed we could see dead bodies scattered over the rocks, and
often we could smell the acrid stench of rotting flesh even at
flight altitude. Occasionally we saw an L-5 liaison plane
directing artillery fire several miles east of the river, but I
never envied those liaison pilots because they were sitting
ducks even more than we were.

"One morning, after I had been using this same pattern
each time I flew over the drop zone, I got the surprise of my
life, and I had no one to blame but myself for my absolute
stupidity. I was flying at treetop level between the hills. I
had slowed down and was ready to begin a shallow bank to
the left when suddenly there was a loud crash which shook
the plane violently. Without pausing to see what had happened, I forgot the drop for a moment and executed the
maneuver known as "getting the hell out of there." There was
no question but that the noise had been caused by a big
Japanese gun.

"Once we were away from the drop zone, the crew chief
inspected the airplane. There was no damage, but the shell
had exploded close. Stupidly I had made all my drop patterns on this target in exactly the same way. Each time I
had used the same approach, and the Japanese on the
ground had quickly figured this out. During the preceding
night, knowing exactly what my pattern would be, they had
moved a fieldpiece into position to be directly under me
when I came lumbering over the next day. It had been
close. They had almost succeeded, and if I had made
another pass they would probably have zeroed in for a sure

kill. This taught me an important lesson in combat, however; the next day I changed my flight path and never again came over the target the same way twice.

"There was another drop area that was almost as tough to find as the one by the dry river bed. This one was located in a dense jungle and there was no clearing to mark the exact spot. As we passed over the area the ground troops would set off a smoke bomb, and I would study the color of the foliage where the smoke rose. Soon I could distinguish that area from the other areas and became so proficient that I could drop accurately even after the smoke gave out. I would approach by an imaginary line that extended from a bare, rocky patch on the mountainside, out over the dropping area, to a cargo ship anchored off the beach. Twice I actually put out the smoke bomb by dropping supplies on top of it. One learned quickly on this type of mission, but I have often wondered what would have happened had the Japs decided to light a smoke bomb at the same time that we first started dropping on this target. I might have flown right over their guns and got my tail shot off. Needless to say, these were chances that had to be taken. We had no choice. The men on the ground fighting for their lives didn't have much of a choice either.

"In addition to our regular drops, we flew a load of supplies to an isolated outpost on the other side of the mountain from Aitape. An Intelligence officer of the 32nd Division went along to help locate the spot. The drop area was in a small clearing in which panels were arranged to aid us in identifying it. After reaching it, we buzzed it to look it over. For some reason—call it intuition if you like—the Intelligence man told me not to drop the supplies. That seemed odd to me, since the panels had been laid out properly, identifying the area as belonging to us.

"We returned to Aitape airstrip. The Intelligence officer had indeed had a vision, and a correct one. The Japanese, just before we arrived at the drop area, had captured it from the Americans and were in full charge. Knowing that the panels were for signaling an airplane, they had left them exactly as the American soldiers had placed them, hoping, of course, to knock us down as we flew over.

"At the end of the third day at Aitape, we were asked to remain for a few more days. Our orders had called for only three days, but I wired Nadzab and was told I could remain. Strange as it may seem, my crew was happy about staying because we could actually see, for a change, just what we were accomplishing toward assisting those weary, battleworn foot soldiers. After having seen how those fellows had to fight and live in the jungles, I thanked God many times that I was a pilot.

"Almost every day C-47s from our squadron and other outfits landed at Aitape, either on missions or en route to or from Hollandia. While my 'Long Island Duck' was being loaded, I contacted several of the pilots and conned them into helping us with a few drops before they returned to their bases. Then I would lead them to the easy drops, point out the drop zone, and take the rough drops myself. It wasn't that I was trying to be brave, but I certainly didn't want to be responsible for those guys getting shot up over a drop zone with which they were unfamiliar.

"I explained to the other crews that they had nothing to worry about—that I was dropping in the places where there were Japanese on the ground shooting at the planes that came in.

"On returning to Aitape after one such drop, one of the pilots called me over to his plane. He pointed to a bullet hole in the cockpit. 'I thought you said there was nothing to these drops', he said, grinning. 'A guy could get hurt doing this!'

"During these missions I begged, borrowed, or stole all the cigarettes I could get and dropped them to the soldiers on the ground. I enclosed a note with each package which said, 'Compliments of the 66th Troop Carrier Squadron.'

"After twelve days of working at this nerve-racking pace, I decided to return to Nadzab. My crew had piled up sixty missions during those days, and all of us had about reached the limits of our endurance. We had dropped over a quarter of a million pounds of supplies and equipment, and the old bird, the faithful old 'Long Island Duck,' was long overdue for maintenance. We were all very tired, but on work like this we had little time to think about ourselves and the physical condition we were in. Our job was to get that load to the ground troops and if *we* were tired, how must they have felt? Since the pilot was responsible for his crew and plane, he had it a bit rougher. And since the rest of the crew were not actively engaged in flying the plane, they had a chance to observe me and must have harbored thoughts about my worn-out condition, and how one simple mistake on my part could wipe us all out. How close they came to having this happen!

"Shortly after we returned to Nadzab, the Commanding General of the 32nd Infantry Division requested that we make a round trip to Aitape. Little did he know that by then I was literally 'out of this world.'

"The next night, after I had returned to Nadzab from Aitape, I was extremely restless and spent most of the night walking around the camp area. My mind was cloudy and the whole operation seemed a fantasy. The next morning I was so exhausted that I could not hold my head up, and it took superhuman strength to speak. Then things seemed to fade, and the last thing I remember was when the flight surgeon came to take me to the hospital.

"The next several months were completely blank to me. I had gradually to learn the simple functions of living as I regained my memory. Finally I could recognize my wife, my family, and friends; and eventually I recovered completely."

George Walker did not tell the authors but he had accomplished one of the most remarkable supply feats of World War II during his days at Aitape. He and his devoted crew and one battered C-47 named "The Long Island Duck" had performed miracles. Though the Japanese didn't know it at the time, five thousand American ground troops had been completely cut off from their source of supply. One over-worked C-47 crew had kept them fighting.

In addition, Walker's airplane was credited with directly saving twenty-six men at River X, so named because its name does not appear on any map. The twenty-six man patrol had been completely surrounded by the Japanese and was slowly running out of ammunition. They had just enough ammunition left to fire an occasional shot at the Japs, but not enough to fight their way out. Walker and his crew dumped the ammo right into the laps of the patrol and the men then fought their way out and survived.

This instance of the part played by Troop Carrier Gooney Birds in the Southwest Pacific is typical of the indispensability of the C-47 during World War II. There is no doubt that the troops stranded beyond the front lines on patrol in New Guinea will never forget the sight of a lone airplane with the old familiar shape circling low over their heads every day bringing emergency provisions.

Any collection of stories about the famous Gooney Bird would not be complete without telling of the time this beautiful, lumbering, defenseless transport became a fighter plane and was officially credited with bringing down an enemy plane. This was just one more "first" in the endless list of aviation firsts claimed by the most famous of air transports.

When this C-47 landed in Italy after a tour of duty in Burma, it had a record that no other C-47 was ever to claim. Some will doubt and dispute this, but it was the only transport airplane in anybody's air force officially credited with downing an enemy fighter airplane. What makes this all the more unusual is that it downed a Japanese *Zero* while actually assigned to support the Fifth Army in Italy!

In a theater of war where Allied fighters and bombers had their sides decorated with swastikas denoting their kills, this old transport brazenly flaunted a small white square with an orange ball in the center—a Japanese flag. The crew chief was the butt of many a joke when the plane taxied up to the ramp at a strange airfield. Such remarks as "Hey,

Sarge, you're fightin' the wrong war," and "You're a little off course, ain't ya, Sarge?" would greet the veteran sergeant as he opened the cargo door and put down the steps. But when the truth came out about the Japanese flag which stood out so boldly on the airplane's side, the jokesters could only stand in awe and shake their heads respectfully. They could hardly believe it but there it was. No one would paint a Japanese flag on an airplane without having downed an enemy airplane. It would be too easy to check the truth of it.

This C-47 officially credited with knocking down the Japanese *Zero* was piloted by Captain Hal M. Scrugham, of Frankfort, Kentucky. His copilot was Lieutenant Elmer J. Jost, of Berwyn, Illinois. The crew and their airplane had been overseas for about two years and had fought their own kind of war through the North African campaign, hauling supplies to the front and taking wounded men back to the rear-line hospitals. That phase of the war had ended, however, when they flew paratroopers to Avellino for a drop in the hills.

It was an urgent call for help from the China-Burma-India Theater of Operations that changed the routine life of Scrugham's C-47. The plane was sent on temporary loan, along with some other C-47s from Africa, to Burma to haul supplies over the Hump.

Two weeks after the airplane arrived in Burma, hardly sufficient time to become familiar with flying conditions over the ragged mountains or the fighting tactics of their new enemy, Scrugham and Jost suddenly found themselves in a tangle to the death with a pair of aggressive *Zeros* determined to add a fat transport to their tally.

"We were flying a routine cargo mission—no passengers—when two *Zeros* jumped us," Scrugham later reported. "I didn't take time to try to figure out what was happening. Instead, I swung the C-47 into a dive and hit the deck as the Japanese fighters peeled off after us for what they thought would be a sure kill.

"The first *Zero* made his pass at us but we were too close

to the ground and he zoomed up without hitting us. The second *Zero* came right down on us. When he got within inches of our airplane I jammed the throttles forward another fraction of an inch and got just a little burst of speed.

"That character must have been trying to ram us because he never swerved. With the added speed I had given my airplane I caused him to miss hitting us dead center, but he didn't miss entirely and we felt the old C-47 shudder for a minute like it was going to shake itself to pieces.

"The Jap plane, after it hit us, kept right on going and we watched it explode as it hit the side of the mountain. We didn't know how much damage it had done to our plane. I moved the elevators first and then the ailerons and found that we had excellent control there. But when I kicked the rudders nothing happened. I knew right then that the Jap had knocked our rudder off. Jost and I looked at each other and talked about climbing as high as we could and bailing out, but I moved the controls some more and, between the elevators and the ailerons, we seemed to be able to control the old bird all right. So we decided to keep right on flying rather than have our airplane suffer the same fate as the Japanese *Zero*.

"Now that I think about it," Scrugham continued, "it never occurred to us to worry about that other *Zero* pilot. We were so scared that his buddy had fixed us up good that we completely forgot about him.

"All my life I guess I'll wonder what ever happened to him. Maybe he thought we had some new kind of secret weapon when he saw us knock down the other *Zero*, and he simply hightailed it for home to report to his superiors. At any rate, he didn't bother us and we never saw him again."

This rugged C-47 was, therefore, officially credited with the downing of one Japanese *Zero*. The veteran Gooney Bird was repaired and was back flying again in a few days. It stayed in the China-Burma-India Theater for two months, flying supplies, and then returned to Italy when the group was ordered to help General Mark Clark's Fifth Army in the Italian campaign.

The DC-3 will do it!

8

The newer planes are faster, more comfortable and have all the latest gadgets on them, but I doubt if any will ever be any more dependable than the old DC-3.

—LUKE CARRUTHERS
Captain, Delta Airlines

THE DC-3 and its predecessors, the DC-1 and DC-2, were originally conceived to be passenger transports for use on the airlines. The demands of the military service soon transformed the DC-3 into a cargo transport, bomber, a fighter, and a flying navigator's classroom. While its versatility in these operations is well-established, not so well known are some of the odd uses to which the Gooney Bird has been put through the years. It has been used as a flying laboratory, a laundry, an airborne battle command post, a flying loudspeaker, spray plane, wire layer, and even as a glider. After its flying days were over, its carcass has been converted into an officers club, a post exchange, and even hoisted to the top of a restaurant to serve as a penthouse for the proprietor's elite customers.

As is traditional with this unique expression of the aeronautical engineer's art, each of these new assignments has constituted a "first," and many have established a precedent for improvements in later aircraft. The Gooney Bird thus parallels the progress of flight in the last three decades; indeed, it has helped to make that progress possible.

On October 15, 1944, a group of Signal Corps experts waited in a small clearing on the western slopes of the Great Smoky Mountains just outside Gatlinburg, Tennessee. They watched the Army Air Forces C-47 approaching fast and low through the smoky-blue haze which was characteristic of the mountains and gave them their name. The C-47 was pointed across the mountains on a course which would normally call for high-altitude flying because of the towering peaks and treacherous air currents ahead. This was a special test mission, however, and the C-47 was hedgehopping across the foothills in defiance of the treacherous downdrafts.

As the plane passed over them and started its climb toward Newfound Gap and the ridgeline, the ground party saw a small white parachute streak from the plane's open door and snap open in the slipstream. As the plane flew on at a carefully calculated 220 feet per second, a tenuous line spiraled out through a tube in the doorway and arched back and down to a connection with the descending parachute.

Men raced to positions beneath the falling line, opening an Army field telephone set as they ran. Leads were snapped onto the line as it fell into their hands. An engineer placed a receiver to his ear. Looks of apprehension crossed the faces of these men whose months of hard work were being weighed in the crucial test.

Tension dissolved completely when the man at the telephone began talking to the engineer in the C-47 which was now disappearing into the blue haze above Newfound Gap.

They were talking through sixteen miles of telephone wire that had just been laid by the airplane.

Talking from airplane to ground was not the important accomplishment; however. To the Air Technical Service Command and its contractor, Bell Telephone Laboratories, the real satisfaction came from laying wire with an airplane. A sixteen-mile length of wire was put down between two ground points over difficult terrain, in perfect condition, in six minutes forty seconds, and a few minutes later the wire could carry a communication. It would have required days to lay the wire over the same rugged course by ground crews.

Halfway around the world, in the China-Burma-India and Pacific theaters, there were mountain ranges far more formidable than the Smokies. There were jungles, head-deep swamps, and other natural obstacles to plague the men who had to provide the Army's vital telephone links. Laying wire across these barriers meant laying it slowly, sometimes from the back of a truck but more often from the back of a man, walking, crawling or swimming.

The Air Force's newly developed air-laying procedure was the answer to these problems. Almost anywhere a line was needed on the ground it could now be laid from the air. More than that, air-laid wire could cross terrain so impenetrable that it could not be crossed on the ground. Also, when laid over this kind of country there was less chance of its being located and cut by the enemy.

From the pilot's viewpoint, there was nothing tricky about flying a wire mission. He would be given the required location of the two ends of the line and advised to fly as low as possible to make certain the wire ends would drop accurately. High speeds and sudden changes of direction had to be carefully avoided, and allowances had to be made for the drift of the wire in crosswinds when passing over the line terminal sites. Outside of these simple factors, there was nothing to it. This was just another case of American ingenuity and persistence being applied to a problem with an airplane that had proved time and time again that it could do the impossible.

There is one tale about the Gooney Bird that, if we stuck strictly to flying, would deprive the plane of part of the history it so richly deserves. It once housed the kitchen that served the best hamburgers in all South Africa.

When Cyril Morley, an Englishman, built a roadhouse near Johannesburg before World War II, he did not plan for the day that his roof might wear out and have to be replaced when material would be scarce. The inevitable happened, of course, and Morley had to scrounge around for anything that would keep the rain off his customers. Wartime shortages included metals, tar paper, and shingles. As time went on, his problem grew worse.

One day he discovered an old C-47 *Dakota*, which had formerly belonged to the RAF, lying in a junk pile not far from his establishment. Being a practical man, Morley purchased the Gooney Bird, hoping that he could use the aluminum for roofing material. He soon discovered, however, that the metal, spot-welded in some places and riveted in others, could not be stripped off intact. Undaunted, Morley secured sufficient help and hoisted the airplane—engines, landing gear, propellers and all—to the roof of his roadhouse.

There it was. The strangest rooftop in all Africa. Cyril Morley's roadhouse became famous and people flocked from miles around to dine in the most distinctive restaurant on the Dark Continent.

After twelve years Cyril Morley sold the C-47 for a fairly good price. The man who had purchased the plane brought a crew of workers who took down the plane and hauled it away. This might be the end of a perfectly good story but it isn't, because somewhere in South Africa the old airplane which was once a rooftop again delivers its passengers and cargo right on schedule.

Lord Louis Mountbatten, Supreme Allied Commander in

Southeast Asia, had troops spread all over that part of the world. To visit each unit or command by ground vehicle was impossible. A C-47 had been assigned to his headquarters and Lord Mountbatten decided to make the C-47 his command post. The C-47 was modified to provide complete living facilities, but the most extensive modification was the installation of an entire radio station in the rear cabin. This enabled Lord Mountbatten to keep in constant contact with his land, sea and air forces.

Today the United States Air Force maintains several flying command posts based on the success of Mountbatten's C-47 command post which first proved that such a system would work.

In order to give the Gooney Bird still more flexibility of operation Air Force engineers were asked to determine the possibility of making it into an amphibian. The new model was to be called a "Dumbo." The crew would have to board the plane via a rope ladder. Pontoons were installed which raised the height of the plane by about twelve feet. When steel stands were put under the pontoons, the airplane reached almost to the ceiling of the plant in Oklahoma City.

The installation of the floats did not change the C-47's flight characteristics. It would still land anywhere a standard C-47 could land because it had four retractable wheels set into the pontoons. There was a rudder to guide it and to brake it in the water, and an anchor was fitted into the left pontoon. Several instruments had to be added to the pilot's panel because the new landing-gear wheels and the pontoon rudder could not be seen from the cockpit.

On the first test of the Dumbo, pilot Dick Richards was a little apprehensive. This was the most drastic modification which had been made on the outside of a C-47 and he wondered if the drag would be prohibitive. Although the airplane had towed gliders successfully, this was different in that the drag of the pontoons might be too great for the power plants, and this drag could not be immediately released should it suddenly try to overcome the pull of the engines.

As Richards lumbered down the runway, the air speed picked up quickly. At flying speed he hauled the Gooney off the ground and found to his surprise that he had used no more than the normal amount of runway for the take-off.

Richards cruised around for a while, using different power settings and flying the airplane in various maneuvers to test its stability, stalling speed, and other characteristics. When the time came to land, he made a normal approach, hit the runway lightly on the rear wheels, and then eased the wheel forward to let the front wheels touch the asphalt. The plane rolled forward as smoothly as if it had been born with floats attached.

The pontoons were 41 feet long—longer than a P-40—five feet wide, and five feet high, and the landing wheels retracted completely into them, thus holding the drag to a minimum. Two doors for the front wheels opened simultaneously with the hydraulic retraction gear, and the rear wheels pulled up neatly into the wells just behind the "step" of each. As could be expected, this extra hydraulic installation caused the whole network of already installed tubing, gauges and valves, and control cables to be changed.

Since a flying boat often hits harder on a water landing than does a land plane on land, the C-47 Dumbo had to be reinforced in its fuselage understructure and in the center wing. Also the temporary rope ladder was later replaced by a permanent ladder with notched steps, closed by hinged flaps, and ran up the side of one of the floats. From here one could climb by means of rungs on the strut to a small door on the side of the fuselage—which was the pilot's escape hatch and the airlines' baggage loading door.

Inside the floats were a series of watertight bulkheads for protection in case the pilot rammed a sunken log or coral reef. The space in the floats was used for gasoline, drawn up to the engines by a newly installed extra fuel pump.

The transformed C-47 proved its adaptability to water, but

only a few of the float type were ever built. The ones that were built simply proved the point that the C-47 could do anything—even swim—if necessary.

World War II was more than a war of armies, navies and air forces pitting their power against each other. It was also a war of logistics, of providing for the buildup and support of military forces by transporting supplies, equipment, and personnel where and when needed. The airplane had made surface means of transportation vulnerable. At the same time, the airplane had given military logisticians the means to provide matériel with a speed and over distances never before possible.

The fabulous Gooney Bird contributed immeasurably to these wartime logistical accomplishments. Its dependability and the great numbers available enabled air transport men to confidently plan large movements by air. The distances of the global war fronts were great, however, and the demands of Allied commanders for logistic support were always greater than the ability of the supply services to satisfy them. New ways to transport supplies by air had to be sought. Could the C-47 tow gliders loaded with supplies just as it had already proven it could tow gliders loaded with troops for air assault operations?

The answer was sought and found by a combined team from the Royal Air Force and the Royal Canadian Air Force. After months of preparation, a giant Waco glider named the "Voo-Doo," with an 84-foot wingspread, was lifted into the air from Montreal by a C-47 *Dakota*. Its destination was England, and the distance: 3,220 miles over the North Atlantic route.

The *Dakota* used on this "Atlantic Sky-glide" mission was piloted by Flight Lieutenant W. S. Longhurst, a Canadian flying with the RAF. The copilot was Flight Lieutenant C. W. H. Thompson. Squadron Leader R. G. Seys, of the RAF, piloted the glider, with Squadron Leader F. M. Goebeil, RCAF, as copilot.

The Voo-Doo lifted a ton and a half of vaccines, radios, and aircraft and engine parts. The *Dakota* was loaded with spare parts and survival equipment, plus extra gas tanks for the long legs of the flight. After 28 hours of flight, most of it in marginal weather, the plane and its glider reached England. But, while the British Air Ministry declared that "the flight opened great new possibilities in air transport," the long-distance haul was not repeated.

Experiments with glider tow methods were conducted throughout the war by the U. S. Army Air Forces. One novel idea was an aerial pickup system whereby a damaged Gooney Bird could be saved from a crash landing and towed back to its base by a companion plane.

A pickup hook was mounted on the left wing tip of the tow plane. This hook was in full view of the pilot. If another plane were disabled, the tow plane could maneuver into position behind the other plane so that the pickup hook would make contact with a 250-foot weighted nylon rope which the crippled plane's crew chief would toss overboard. The hook on the wing of the tow plane was held in place by a soft aluminum pin which would break off when the contact was made and swing out behind a conventional glider tow release mechanism. Thus, the tow plane could release the disabled craft just as it would cut loose a glider.

No radio communication between the planes was needed, and all the pilot of the disabled plane was required to do was to maintain a straight and level course. If the speed of the planes was correct—no more than 5 miles per hour difference between them—the elasticity of the nylon rope would absorb the shock.

The system was first tried in April 1945, at the Clinton County Army Airfield at Wilmington, Ohio, with two C-47s, one of which played "wounded" by cutting out one engine. A standard glider tow release was located below the fuselage near the center of the wing, and the nylon rope was stowed inside a dural sleeve that acted as a stabilizer during trailing. The other C-47, which had the pickup hook on its wing tip, maneuvered into position, made contact with the dangling rope and continued on its flight towing the other ship behind it.

After the initial try, many successful pickups were made, including one in which a C-47 had both engines shut off and propellers feathered. The originators of the idea, Glider Branch engineers of the Air Technical Service Command Aircraft Laboratory, believed that the system could be used on any type of aircraft including the heaviest of bombers. However, although another "first" for the C-47, this unique idea was never used in a combat operation.

Residents around this same Wilmington, Ohio, Army air base were startled, one spring day in 1945, to see a Gooney Bird without engines or propellers gliding and banking in the morning sun and then gracefully coming to rest on the nearby Clinton County Army Airfield. The next day they saw two Gooneys hitched together towing a large transport-type glider. The residents did not know it but they were watching experiments designed to see if freight could be shipped by glider express after the war was over.

What the Wilmington citizenry had witnessed was a conventional transport made into a glider, and the first "tandem tow," in which two airplanes hauled a huge glider into the air.

The Army Air Forces had already developed several models of gliders to carry airborne troopers on invasion missions. All these gliders, however, were developed for towing behind twin-engined airplanes, generally the standard work horse of the Troop Carrier Command—the old reliable Douglas C-47 *Skytrain*.

But air transport was gradually moving from twin-engined to four-engined planes, and the Air Transport Command began getting the larger Douglas C-54 for their world-wide airline.

At Wright Field, Dayton, Ohio, headquarters of the Air Technical Service Command, it was decided to develop a glider suitable as a "Skytrailer" for the much bigger and faster C-54 *Skymaster* and to have that glider ready for the time when the Troop Carrier Command would change from twin-engine to four-engine operation. None of the existing gliders could meet the specifications for this.

The problem was tossed into the laps of engineers of the Glider Branch of the Aircraft Laboratory with headquarters at Wright Field.

"We started by figuring the reserve power available in the C-54, and determined a desired cruising speed for plane and glider," said Major William C. Lazarus, acting chief of the Glider Branch. "Then we began to conceive a purely theoretical design and configuration of a glider which would meet the requirements.

"As the specifications for this glider evolved from the drafting boards and slide rules, it became more and more obvious that the size and gross weight of the glider we wanted would coincide with that of the airplane we had been using as a tow ship—the Douglas C-47.

The project engineer assigned to the study was Captain Bernard J. Driscoll, who was not only an aeronautical engineer, but also a qualified glider test pilot. Working with him was Captain Chester Decker, who in prewar days had been one of America's leading sailplane experts.

"It has never been done—but let's take the C-47, jerk out its engines and see if it will prove to be the glider we have been trying to design," Decker suggested. As a glider pilot he knew that the C-47 would be a safe and maneuverable glider, and he believed it would meet the tests.

The enthusiasm of Decker and Driscoll for converting the C-47 into a glider quickly communicated itself to their superiors and they were told to go ahead with their experiments. Although no one had ever converted a plane of this size into a glider, the plan offered another possible use for an aircraft already in production that had proved itself on every battlefront. Much time and money could be saved by converting an already existing airplane rather than designing and building a completely new glider.

The moment that Brigadier General Franklin O. Carroll, Chief of the Air Technical Service Command engineering division, gave permission to proceed with the project there immediately arose an argument between the power pilots and the glider pilots.

Could a 26,000-pound airliner be denuded of engines and handled safely by the average glider pilot?

The power boys doubted that any pilot could "dead-stick" a transport with sufficient accuracy to make it a successful glider. They believed that the rate of descent of the power-less plane would be so great there would be no time to judge a landing approach. On the other hand, the glider pilots pointed out that with such a relatively clean glider, as the C-47 undoubtedly would be, the distance to be covered on the glide would be greater than in the powered plane and therefore the pilot would have more time to select his landing place.

Aeronautical engineers, agreeing with the glider advocates, pointed out that it would require less power to pull the C-47 in level flight than to pull the conventional glider, which lacked the clean lines of the C-47.

Tests were started at the glider experiment station at Wilmington. A C-47 airplane with only fuel and crew aboard took off and flew to 5,000 feet where both its engines were cut and the plane dead-sticked to a landing time and time again. Pilots who flew the airplane on these tests were Captains Decker, Santmeyer and Rintoul, the last two were former airline pilots with more than 5,000 flying hours each.

As the experiments progressed, the altitude where the engines were cut off was gradually lowered until the pilots were gliding the C-47 in from 2,000 feet. Soon everyone was convinced that the C-47 could glide in and hit the spot consistently regardless of winds and the amount of load, provided that the pilots were qualified.

The next problem was to determine if the C-47 had sufficient control when being towed as a glider.

"In general, being towed in flight is far less stable than

free gliding or powered flight," Major Lazarus explained. "All gliders, while in tow, require the constant attention of the glider pilot. For example, when a wing goes down in a gust, the glider pilot must quickly bring it up. Otherwise the wing may get so far down he may not have sufficient control to pull it up again. A glider without adequate control and thus displaced will continue to roll at the end of the tow rope and the only solution is to cut loose from the tow ship. Once in free flight the glider can quickly be righted, of course, but cutting loose means a forced landing.

"All Army Air Force gliders up to this point have been high-winged monoplanes and have been designed specifically as gliders with more aileron, elevator and rudder control than the conventional airplane. Here was a C-47, designed to be flown only as a powered airplane. Would it stand the test at the end of a nylon tow rope?

"Before we could find the answer to this question the engineers had a problem to solve. Where would we attach the tow rope? The pull of a tow rope tugging along a 26,000-pound glider through rough air is no small item. A huddle was called one morning on this problem with drawings of the C-47 cluttering the big conference table. And there right in front of us on the drawing board we found the answer.

"The versatile C-47 had built into it the solution to even this knotty problem. Douglas engineers, who had never dreamed of towing when they designed the airplane back in 1933, had provided a rectangular inspection door on the belly of the plane through which mechanics could readily examine the main wing structure where it passed beneath the fuselage.

"The hitch could be made by simply unbolting this inspection panel and replacing it with one specially fitted with a tow release mechanism. Further, it could be done on a C-47 without removing the engines. The rope would not interfere with the props and, since the glider or towed airplane always flies slightly over the tow plane, the rope would not rub against or damage the nose.

"The tow hitch attachment was quickly designed and installed on the belly of a C-47 at the field near Wilmington. We were now ready to proceed with the next step in the creation of what was to become the XCG-17, the biggest payload glider, carrying in excess of seven tons."

With Santmeyer, Rintoul, and Decker doing the flying, flight tests were begun. The first time the two C-47s were hitched together with a standard nylon rope 350 feet long. This flight was made to determine the handling characteristics of the C-47 when in towed flight and to test the tow hitch mechanism. The lead C-47 took up slack and applied take-off power. The towed C-47 applied power but not quite as much as the tow plane, so that the tow rope remained taut. Down the runway the two airplanes came, up went the towing C-47 and then the towed ship.

When the two ships gained safe altitudes the second C-47 cut its engines and feathered its props. It was now in full towed flight. It handled beautifully. Shortly afterward it was cut loose and glided safely in for a landing.

"We were quick to recognize that we had something else besides a new glider," said Major Lazarus. "Here was a worthwhile by-product of the XCG-17 development. Here was the making of a 'tandem tow.' For months, as the gliders became larger and heavier, the need for the assisted take-off of the tow plane and glider had been felt. The power of one airplane was sufficient for level flight once the desired altitude had been gained, but extra power was needed for the climb.

"Could two airplanes be coupled together tandem just as two locomotives are coupled together to pull heavy trains up steep mountain grades? Could a heavy glider be attached behind two C-47s? True, this was a digression from the primary objective of developing the XCG-17, but it would help solve one of our problems, so we went ahead."

The first tandem tow was made using two C-47s pulling a standard fifteen-place CG-4A, one of the smaller gliders. This was not much of a load for two airplanes, but it was done to determine the effect of the ropes on both the front and the back of the middle airplane. Pilots were surprised to find that the tandem tow was easy, even though it looked like a circus stunt. Later the two C-47s in tandem took off with a loaded XCG-10A, one of the Army's largest gliders in tow. At altitude, the lead C-47 cut loose and the other C-47 continued to tow the big glider. One C-47 could not have taken the loaded XCG-10A off the ground. Here was the first real "Skytrain." Here for the first time was opened up vast new possibilities for air cargo development.

These tests completed, the next step was to convert a C-47 into a glider. General Carroll imposed only one restriction: He assigned a war-weary C-47 recently returned from a combat theater to the experimenters, but he ordered that the airplane should not be so stripped that it could not be restored as a normal airplane if the experiments were not successful.

The Glider Branch accepted the plane gratefully and proceeded to tear out hundreds of pounds of weight. The radio operator's and forward baggage compartments were eliminated and a new floor added so that cargo could be loaded farther forward to compensate for the loss of forward weight when the engines were removed. The engines were taken off and hemispherical streamlined noses were added to the nacelles to reduce drag.

The first flights of the C-47 that had become the XCG-17 were made at the Clinton County Army Airfield in the summer of 1944. At the controls was Major D. O. Dodd.

"The flights were as successful as had been expected," Major Lazarus explained. "The glider engineers had been slightly concerned that some small amount of ballast might be needed to fly the glider in the lightweight condition. On the first flight about 400 pounds of lead shot were added in the nose to insure that the G-17 would not be tail-heavy. After the first few flights it was proved that even this was not necessary."

The XCG-17 was America's largest glider at that time and

the only cargo glider that required no ballast when flown in minimum-weight condition. It had a long flat glide angle—a ratio of 14 to 1, which meant that it could go forward fourteen feet while dropping only one foot. By comparison, the small CG-4 glider had a glide ratio of ten or twelve to one. The XCG-17 had a remarkably low stalling speed of 35 miles an hour as compared to the 55-mile-an-hour stalling speed of the CG-4. And, most important of all, it could be towed as fast as 270 to 290 miles per hour, whereas the top speed of the conventional glider was only 200 miles per hour.

And so one more accomplishment was added to the long and never-ending list of tasks the indestructible Gooney Bird had been asked to perform. No other airplane or air vehicle in the history of flight can match it. Whatever the requirement, whatever the job, the DC-3 could do it!

The Vietnam experience

9

In an age of supersonic jet aircraft, megaton atomic weapons and sophisticated electronic devices, nothing seemed quite so incongruous as a lumbering C-47 transport evolving into a potent weapon system. Counterinsurgency warfare, as exemplified by the Southeast Asian war, had generated modern air weaponry paradoxes such as old T-28 trainers serving as attack aircraft. The gunship joined this group as an improvisation that surprised nearly everyone. From a humble modification of the apparently ageless C-47 (DC-3), the gunship grew into a highly complex weapon system. In doing so, it pioneered new research developments and revolutionized aerial counterinsurgency tactics.

—Lt. Col. Jack S. Ballard
Historian U.S. Air Force

There seems to be no doubt that future historians will label U.S. involvement in the Vietnamese war the most agonizing ever experienced by its military forces. For over a decade American forces were required to support the South Vietnamese government by supplying, first, advisors, then gradually increasing military materiel and manpower which eventually numbered more than half a million men.

As the Air Force was committed to sending flying units to Southeast Asia beginning in June 1962, it was probably inevitable that the venerable C-47 Gooney Bird would have a role to play. There were several hundred of them still in the flying inventory or in storage. Although the Air Force had been preparing for nuclear warfare, once more it had to develop a force capable of supporting ground forces operating in a jungle environment.

The concept developed was labeled "counterinsurgency" and aircraft and tactics were conceived for the waging of guerilla-type warfare. The Gooney Bird was immediately called on to do its usual job of flying U.S. and South Vietnamese forces to battle zones and keeping them supplied with air-dropped food, medicines and ammunition.

Contrary to popular forecasts, the war did not end quickly. It dragged on month after month as a determined enemy, willing to fight for a hundred years if necessary, stayed in the jungle and infiltrated the entire country. U.S. air and ground forces with weapon systems designed for the nuclear age were relatively ineffective against jungle troops who fought a conventional war in their own country without uniforms but with a seemingly unlimited supply of arms and ammunition.

As always in modern wars, weapons research and technology accelerated during the Vietnam war years. This was particularly evident in the area of tactical intelligence. Using a variety of aircraft and sensors, U.S. tactical reconnaissance forces were gradually able to collect information, process and interpret photographs within ever-decreasing time-spans so that air and ground commanders could take appropriate decisive actions. Gooney Birds, given the designation of EC-47 (for electronic-equipped), were fitted out with a variety of optical, radar and electronic sensors as well as cameras for reconnaissance. The photographic reconnaissance included the use of laser beams and photo cartridges to illuminate target areas at night. Electronic devices were used to locate and analyze enemy devices emitting electromagnetic radiation. Infrared cameras were installed in a number of EC-47s to record areas or objects that emitted thermal (heat) radiations. Radar was used to record either fixed or moving targets by detecting the radar echo of enemy troop concentrations.

Such jobs were easily accomplished by the ageless Gooney. It had done most of them before in other wars. While the equipment on board was now more sophisticated, the faithful aerial workhorse had the same airframe and engines it always had. There was nothing spectacular about the aircraft or its surveillance mission. It surprised no one that the Gooney Bird, obsolescent by standards applied to every other aircraft in the world, would be doing its part in this latest war.

But the Gooney's greatest role, however, was yet to come. The lumbering C-47 was to grow into what one Air Force historian called "a potent, highly complex weapon system." Despite its age, it was to be called upon to pioneer and revolutionize aerial counterinsurgency tactics in the jet area. And it was to take on an entirely new designation—AC-47 (for attack version)—and new nicknames—"Puff, the Magic Dragon" and "Spooky."

The new role in the never-ending saga of the DC-3 grew out of the simple fact that the first-line combat aircraft of the U.S. Air Force of the early 1960s too often could not find nor accurately strike enemy targets at night or under cover of a dense jungle canopy. As the success of guerrilla warfare against the sophisticated firepower of the United States was proven daily in Vietnam, it became obvious that not only must the enemy forces be detected, but a great amount of firepower had to be brought to bear quickly on them before they could slip away using the twin shields of darkness and the jungle. What was needed was an aircraft that had the range to cover any area in South Vietnam, loiter for hours awaiting calls for assistance from friendly ground forces, carry many pounds of the latest electronic detection equipment and then have the capability to remain in the target area and place devastating firepower down on a precise, limited section of the jungle. What was required was a gunship—something akin to the Navy's old battleship—that could rain down overwhelming firepower exactly where it was needed. What was *not* needed was a supersonic jet fighter plane.

The need, quickly recognized on the battlefield, was not so quickly fulfilled. The answer evolved as the product of several men whose greatest task turned out to be not so much as arriving at a solution to the problem but convincing those in authority that they had truly arrived at a solution and could prove it.

Credited with being the first to propose a way to counter the threat in South Vietnam was Ralph E. Flexman who, as an engineer for Bell Aerosystems Co., became intensely interested in the problems of limited warfare due to his company's involvement in the development of special hardware for use in Southeast Asia. Coincidentally, he held a Mobilization Day assignment as an Air Force major with the Behavioral Sciences Laboratory at Wright-Patterson Air Force Base, Ohio. In a summary of several ideas he and his Bell Aerosystems colleagues were working on, he reported to his reserve military superior, "with respect to aircraft, we believe that lateral firing, while making a pylon turn, will prove effective in controlling ground fire from many AA (antiaircraft) units. In theory at least, this should more than triple the efficiency of conventional aircraft on reconnaissance and destructive missions."

Actually, Flexman's basic suggestion was not totally new. Machine guns had been mounted on World War I aircraft so they could be fired laterally by gunners at air and ground targets. Experiments were later conducted at Brooks Field, Texas in 1926–27 in a DeHavilland-4. As noted in an earlier chapter, side-firing .50 caliber machine guns were mounted in aircraft of the 443rd Troop Carrier Group supporting British forces against the Japanese in Burma during World War II.

The concept of firing side-firing guns while in a pylon turn had not surfaced since the Brooks Field experiments when Lt. Fred Nelson flew pylon turns, sighted a ground target through an aiming device on a wing strut and scored hits with his .30 caliber machine gun. What had inspired Flexman was an article he had read about a South American missionary, Nate Saint, who had perfected delivery of mail and supplies to the remote villages of Arica Indian tribes by lowering a bucket on a long rope. As he made a pylon turn, the bucket would hover over a point on the ground where natives could pick out the contents.

Flexman also recalled his own experiences as a flight instructor when he was required to teach his students how to pivot an aircraft around a telephone pole or a fence post while they held them in view at the tip of a wing. As Air Force historian Lt. Col. Jack S. Ballard recorded in his excellent study of the use of fixed-wing gunships in Vietnam: "He therefore believed it reasonable that with a very small sight one could fire ammunition along the sight path to a target. All this pointed to possible counterinsurgency applications."

Despite Flexman's tying the idea together, it was his contact with Gilmour C. MacDonald, now a retired Air Force colonel, that was most influential in the development of the gunship. In April 1942, while Allied shipping losses were extremely high, MacDonald, then a First Lieutenant in the Coast Artillery, suggested a way to increase the effectiveness of civilian aircraft on submarine patrol. He wrote to his superiors, "With a view of providing means for continuous fire upon submarines forced to the surface, it is proposed that a fixed machine gun be mounted transversely in the aircraft so that by flying a continually banked circle the pilot may keep the underseacraft under continuous fire if necessary." Unfortunately, MacDonald's proposal fell on deaf ears.

In 1961 as an Air Force lieutenant colonel, MacDonald resurrected his idea and proposed it to the Tactical Air Command. He wrote, "by flying a banked circle, the airplane can keep the gun pointed continuously at a target, and by flying along with one wing low, limited longitudinal strafing can be done without worrying about pullout." Again, his suggestion was ignored.

At a fortuitous meeting of Flexman and MacDonald in late 1961, the former learned of the latter's recommendations and of the Nate Smith mail delivery successes in South America. By 1963 Flexman was convinced that the basic idea had considerable merit. As he saw it, there were three main areas that should be investigated. As the Air Force history states, these were "ballistics of the projectiles as they were fired and their dispersion; ability of the pilot to aim his lateral weapon and hold the target; and the reaction time necessary to change from straight-and-level flight to an on-pylon turn."

Flexman, not on active duty, suggested to Captain John C. Simons that a test program should be formally begun to answer the three questions he posed. Simons, as a research psychologist and pilot on active duty with the Aerospace Medical Laboratory at Wright-Patterson Air Force Base, was convinced that Flexman's idea was workable and diligently pursued it through his official channels. He proposed a nine-month study to include test flights to verify the concept but was rebuffed. However, as the official Air Force history states, "one of his superiors gave him under-the-table approval for a few test flights." These flights were conducted both day and night in a T-28 trainer with a makeshift sight (a grease-pencilled line on the left cockpit window) at altitudes between 500 and 3,000 feet. "He marveled at the pylon turn's simplicity and the ease with which a target could be acquired and held in the sight," according to the history. These tests by Simons were confirmed by flights in a C-130 cargo aircraft where tracking targets such as trucks, silos, barns, moving horses and even fighting geese proved easy both from the standpoint of flying and sighting.

To prove how "easy" it was, Simons conducted tests with three synchronized cameras—one to record the pilot's sight alignment, another fixed on the instrument panel, and the third in the cargo compartment where a side-firing gun might be positioned. The success he demonstrated eventually resulted in approval for official flight tests but only after frustrating delays due to lack of priority, funds and skepticism of the project at higher levels than Simons and his colleagues.

Simons was transferred and it fell to Capt. Ronald W. Terry, a Vietnam combat veteran, to carry on in late 1963. Having flown fighters in Vietnam, he knew firsthand how difficult it was to find and fire on a ground target in bad weather, at night and when under intense ground fire. Once he became aware of what had gone before and now assigned to the Laboratory, Terry decided that his role had to be that of salesman because he was convinced that the project was worthwhile. He drafted a scenario showing how a side-firing weapon system could be used mainly for the defense of South Vietnamese hamlets and forts. By the summer of 1964, Terry had won his case and tests were begun in Florida using a C-131 transport.

At this time, members of the 1st Combat Applications Group were conducting tests with equipment and tactics for counter-insurgency operations using C-47 aircraft. They asked for and were given permission to install and test three rapid-firing Gatling "miniguns" in one of the Gooneys. These tests were immediately successful but official sanction of the idea was still far off. There was still much skepticism at higher command levels about the idea of a slow cargo plane being resurrected for the proposed combat job.

Admittedly, the Gooney was vulnerable to ground fire and interception by enemy aircraft, but the advantages of using the C-47 included its availability in large numbers, along with the crews to fly them. It could carry a large volume of ammunition and flares and could remain on alert and over a target area for long periods of time. The crew could arm, disarm, maintain and repair weapons in flight and assess the battle situation before and immediately after an attack. As to its vulnerability, Terry argued that the C-47 could fly above the range of enemy small arms fire and there were no enemy aircraft to intercept them. "Certainly," he told his doubters, "the C-47 is bound to be less vulnerable than the Army's helicopters" which by that time in 1964 were being used extensively as gunships.

Captain Terry's arguments eventually prevailed and the order came down from Chief of Staff Curtis E. LeMay to test the Gatling-equipped C-47 in combat. Upon arrival in Vietnam, a new advantage of using the C-47 as a ground attack weapon system surfaced. It was discovered that its great slant range gave it the capability to strike targets on steep mountain slopes or in other previously inaccessible spots. It was during these initial tests that the first new nickname for the C-47 originated. The Air Force history explains:

"The (C-47) gunship fired tracer ammunition on night missions to see where the minigun rounds were hitting. The guns' rapid fire appeared as tongues of flame spewing from the black sky accompanied by a distinctive sound. An impressive sight, it boosted the morale of fort and hamlet defenders but terrorized the enemy. It didn't take long for the AC-47 to earn the nicknames of 'Puff, the Magic Dragon' and 'dragonship.'"

Terry believes the name derived from the fact that 1964 was the Chinese Year of the Dragon and coincidentally from stories from captured enemy prisoners about the tongues of fire from the gunship, and recollections of the child's fairy tale, *Puff, the Magic Dragon*. Others trace it to the child's song, popular in 1964, about a magic dragon.

The nickname was unimportant but it drew renewed interest in the Gooney Bird in a strong military role. Reports from Vietnam about its success prompted one Air Force general to report that not only was it an exceptionally useful weapon but that it had a concurrent great psychological impact "way out of proportion to effectiveness of other aircraft strike efforts and ground force efforts." The result was the assignment of the first 16-plane AC-47 squadron to South Vietnam in mid-1965. With typical Yankee ingenuity, a relatively ancient aircraft had been adapted to take part in still another war.

As historian Jack Ballard wrote, the idea of using the Gooney Bird in an entirely new role had traveled a "tortuous path." The proposal had almost died on several occasions. "It faced bureaucratic oblivion," he said, "burial in government files, rejection by ballistic experts, plus the usual delaying problems of time, manpower and money. Only the dogged persistence of key individuals enabled the concept to emerge from such a deadly thicket." He gave credit to the four mentioned here as deserving of being remembered—MacDonald as the originator, Flexman as the catalyst, Simons as the tester and Terry as the seller of the idea. Ballard concludes: "Their evolutionary efforts combined to create what was probably the most unique weapon system employed in Southeast Asia—the gunship."

The AC-47 deserved the plaudits it received. In the months following its introduction in 1965 with the 1st, 4th and, later, the 14th Air Commando Squadrons, the aircraft pulled out of mothballs flew hundreds of armed reconnaissance missions, not only in South Vietnam but Laos and Thailand as well with outstanding results. These missions, which earned a new nickname of "Spooky," were flown around the clock and continually demonstrated the plane's versatility for the next four years. They performed a wide variety of tasks from leaflet dropping and other psychological warfare missions to flying protective cover for friendly truck convoys and destruction of those not so friendly.

The year 1969 saw the end of the use of AC-47s in the hands of U.S. pilots. During the four years of their use as gunships, the 53 AC-47s assigned had successfully defended 3,926 hamlets, outposts and forts, according to official statistics. In doing so, the crews were able to boast that "no outpost or village was ever lost while under gunship protection." About a dozen of them had been downed or severely damaged late in the four-year period by Soviet-made antiaircraft rockets.

The AC-47s phased out of American hands but not out of the war. Other transports—Fairchild C-119s and Lockheed C-130s—were outfitted with Gatlings and took over the chore. The AC-47s were transferred to South Vietnamese, Laotian and Thai units and continued their special missions.

It was probably inevitable that the Spooky flare and gunship missions would have their heroes because of the risk involved. Although many crew members won the Distinguished Flying Cross and the Air Medal for valor in combat, one of their number was awarded America's highest decoration—the Medal of Honor. His name: Airman First Class John L. Levitow.

On the night of February 24, 1969, Levitow climbed aboard his assigned AC-47, codenamed Spooky 71, for a combat air patrol over the Saigon area. After 4½ hours of inactivity, Major Ken Carpenter, aircraft commander, was vectored toward Bien Hoa where a U.S. Army base was under attack by a large enemy force. The official Air Force report tells the story:

"As Spooky 71 turned to meet the enemy, the pilot and copilot spotted muzzle flashes on the southern and eastern perimeters of Long Binh Army Base. With hot activity below, they moved into attack orbit and fired about 3,000 rounds. After the second pass, they were directed to give the ground troops more flare illumination and to remain over the area.

"In the cargo compartment, Spooky 71's loadmaster, A1C John

L. Levitow, was busily setting ejection and ignition controls on the 2-million candlepower magnesium flares. He would carefully hand the flares to one of the gunners, Sgt. Ellis C. Owen, who hooked them onto the lanyard. The sound of mortar fire rose above the engine noise. A turn of the aircraft indicated the pilot was fixing on a new target. Then came the sudden shock of a blast, a white flash, showers of flying metal, and the sinking sensation of the aircraft veering sharply right and down. Crewmembers in the rear of the aircraft were thrown violently about and injured. Unknown to the crew at the time, a North Vietnamese Army 82-mm mortar shell had hit Spooky 71's right wing.

"At the moment of the blast, Sergeant Owen had one finger through the safety pin ring preparatory to dropping a flare. Knocked from his hand, the armed flare rolled on the floor. The crew knew it took but 20 seconds for the flare to ignite. They also knew the consequences of an ignited flare on board—the 4,000° Fahrenheit burn and the incapacitating toxic smoke. In that instant of crisis, A1C Levitow, severely injured with shrapnel in his right side, was dragging himself to the open cargo door to pull away one of his injured comrades. Suddenly he saw the armed flare for the first time. It was rolling between number one minigun and a jumble of spilled ammunition and storage cans. Filled with terror at the sight of the smoking flare, Levitow knew he had to get it out at once or all would be lost.

"Moving in pain and with great difficulty in the pitching gunship he finally reached the flare. He grasped it and crawled slowly but determinedly to the open door. At last he pushed the flare out; it ignited almost instantly.

"Major Carpenter regained control of the aircraft and managed to get it and the injured crew back to Bien Hoa Air Base. Later he said, 'It is my belief that this story could not have been told by any other member of my crew had Levitow failed to perform his heroic action.'"

There were not many more U.S. Air Force AC-47 missions after this heroic action by Airman Levitow. The flight of Spooky 71 was a fitting climax to four years of intense flying of aircraft that were now a quarter century old—way past their prime by every known standard. To people who know and love the ubiquitous Gooney Bird, it was no surprise—just further proof that this faithful machine does not live by the rules set for other of man's contrivances.

The legend goes on and on

10

We badly need an aircraft which will provide the DC-3's reliability, its same ease of maintenance, and a similar low cost. One approach could be to marry a modern turboprop engine to a modern airframe. Surely our design capabilities are great enough to create a plane as advanced . . . as the DC-3 was in its day.

> —SENATOR A. S. ("MIKE") MONRONEY
> Former Chairman, Senate Aviation Subcommittee

THERE WERE over 10,000 DC-3s and their military counterparts manufactured between 1936 and 1946. Today, more than thirty years after the last Gooney Bird rolled out of the Douglas hangar, 2,500 of them are still flying around the world. The first DC-3 to come off the Douglas production line on June 28, 1936, was last reported flying for the Pacific Lumber Company of San Francisco. The second one, produced on July 10, 1936, was owned by Ozark Airlines, which purchased it in September 1950 from American Airlines, the original owner. Ozark's vice president,

Francis M. Higgins, reported that this veteran had logged over 50,000 hours of flight time, had been overhauled six times, had been powered by fifty sets of engines, and had undergone all kinds of updating modifications before it was eventually sold in the late 1960s.

A North Central Airlines DC-3, now in the Ford Museum at Dearborn, Michigan, lays claim to the fact that it has flown more hours than any other aircraft in history. Before its arrival for permanent display, it had logged over 84,000 hours—more than nine years aloft! It had flown more than 12 million air miles, had worn out 550 main gear tires and 68 pairs of engines and had consumed more than eight million gallons of fuel. The best statistic of all is that it had never been involved in even a minor accident in all its years of service.

No one would have dared predict that the venerable Gooney which had done so much for the war effort would also have an impact on postwar aviation. The impetus given to aeronautics during the war years brought forth great promise for the future of aviation. "In a short time," the experts said, "the DC-3 will be replaced by newer, faster jet transports and will go to the boneyard like the Stinsons, Boeings, and Fords of yesteryear."

The experts were wrong. True, great advancements in aircraft performance have been made. Jets replaced piston engines, and transoceanic flights from the United States to Europe and the Orient are so commonplace that the world might be tempted to forget planes as slow and as old-fashioned in design as the DC-3. But no one reckoned with the astonishing tenacity of the Gooney Bird at staying in the air, and this includes the Civil Aeronautics Board, which in 1942 decreed it could not certify the airworthiness of DC-3s to carry passengers past 1947. The deadline was extended year after year until finally, in 1953, the board declared that, in the future, there would be no limitation on any DC-3 that could pass the routine inspections.

The U.S. Air Force and the U.S. Navy, as well as the flying arms of many other nations, planned to replace their aging Gooney Birds as soon as more modern transports became available. Today, the military versions of the Gooney still squat on the ramps of the world's airfields and plod the international airways far beneath the contrails of the sleek jets.

Following the Second World War, surplus C-47s glutted the used airplane market. Twelve hundred dollars and a pilot's license were all that was needed to put an ex-military pilot into the airline business. Although Douglas had discontinued production of the DC-3, thousands of requests for spare parts were being received. Potential operators asked about modifying the austere bucket-seat models into comfortable commercial versions. Douglas decided to market its own improvements in a faster version— the Super DC-3. Three and a half feet longer than the original from which it was derived, more powerful engines, squared-off wing tips, and more streamlined cowling and wheel fairings boosted the speed to about 200 mph with a load of over thirty passengers. The Douglas promoters proudly announced that the Super DC-3 was "capable of carrying on indefatigably in the noble tradition of its famous ancestor," but the face lifting didn't prove exciting. The U.S. Navy procured one hundred and one, which were designated as R4D-8s, but orders from other customers totaled only three. Potential users of the Gooney preferred the plain DC-3 without the added frills.

In seeking ways to improve the DC-3, many innovations have been tried. British European Airways Corporation decided that the old shape was all right, but that the engine sound needed changing. A new note was added, high-pitched and shrill, which is characteristic of the turboprop engine. B.E.A. wanted to try the Rolls-Royce Dart engines in two of their DC-3s to test engine performance of the Darts as well as to see if the planes would deliver more air speed and power.

A newcomer to civil aviation, the turboprop arrived on the scene after World War II without the backlog of military experience which, in the past, had proved to be invaluable in launching new engines—whether piston or jet—on commercial carriers. Relatively little was then known of the problems that turboprop operation would impose on the civil operator.

The answers to the problems of ground handling, maintenance, operating techniques, and traffic control seemed to lie in fitting the engine to a thoroughly proved airframe, getting in as much flying time as possible with the resulting combination, and doing all this as cheaply as possible. The only airplane in the world with a "thoroughly proved" airframe was the DC-3.

Conversion was accomplished at Hucknall, England, with only minor difficulties. The result was an aircraft with a maximum gross weight of 28,000 pounds, a cruising speed of 202 miles per hour at 25,000 feet, and a fuel consumption of 120 imperial gallons per hour.

It was decided that the airplane should be used on a regular freight run so that there would be some revenue resulting from the testing program. Accordingly, on August 15, 1951, a regular freight service was set up between London and Hanover and later between London, Copenhagen, Paris, and Milan.

Interesting developments cropped up as the tests were being conducted. It was found, for example, that there had to be certain restrictions on freight. An ear-shattering explosion can occur from a bottle of champagne in an unpressurized cabin at 25,000 feet. It was quickly found that the turboprop version of the DC-3 couldn't carry bottled goods, livestock or fresh fruit at the most fuel-efficient altitudes for the engines.

How did the pilots like the "new" DC-3? They loved it. The engine proved very satisfactory from the maintenance point of view and was remarkably free of the minor troubles caused by vibration which plague the piston engine. Mechanics liked it because it was easily accessible and oil consumption was low. Flight crews and passengers liked it in flight because it gave a smooth ride and was exceptionally free of vibration in the air. Once again, the unbelievable had happened. The Gooney Bird had scored another aviation "first." However, it remained for Jack Conroy and his Tri-Turbo Three to bring the concept to economic fruition 25 years later.

It was midnight. An Eastern Air Lines maintenance crew was checking out a *Constellation* for its regular flight to Miami. Inside the Maintenance office, a foreman reached up to the calendar over his desk, tore off the page marked "November 21, 1956," and threw it into the waste basket. Looking into his notebook, he checked an entry and called out, "Hey! Ready to go on your midnight ride?"

"All set," a man replied. "Two men will ride in the cockpit and two on the tug. The police will meet us at the gate. I'll call you when I get her delivered."

"Okay," the foreman answered.

The gates at the southern end of Washington National Airport were pushed open and policemen were waiting on their motorcycles. Out of the Eastern Air Lines hangar rolled a wingless and engineless DC-3 being towed, tail first, by an airplane tug. The man on the tug chugged along cautiously and angled for the gate. The policemen started up their motorcycles and went ahead to stop traffic outside one of the nation's busiest air terminals.

The old crate was being taken to the National Air Museum because Dr. Paul Garber, museum curator, knew what the DC-3 had done in the past. In 1948, Dr. Garber had written to Eddie Rickenbacker and suggested that Eastern Air Lines should earmark one of its DC-3s for Air Museum purposes, preferably one with an exceptional war record and commercial performance.

Rickenbacker agreed. He selected a veteran which had flown over eight and one-half million miles and carried 213,000 passengers since its maiden flight in 1937. It had averaged ten and one-half hours per day in service and had seen more than its share of thunderstorms, cranky passengers, and rough runways.

Appropriately, the official presentation was made in 1953 during the celebration of the fiftieth anniversary of the Wright brothers' first successful flight at Kitty Hawk. It became the 163rd exhibit given to the Air Museum and is especially treasured by Dr. Garber because it is "a wonderful example of the longevity and adaptability of the transport airplane. The DC-3 has an eternal place in aviation history." It enjoys a place of honor today permanently suspended in the National Air and Space Museum's air transportation exhibit area.

At the bottom of the world on October 31, 1956, a lone R4D,

Navy version of the DC-3, flew to the South Pole and landed. Piloted by Commander Gus Shinn, with Captain William "Trigger" Hawkes as copilot and Admiral George J. Dufek, leader of Operation Deep Freeze I, as one of the passengers, the *Que Será Será*—"what is to be, will be"—fought its way from McMurdo Sound and touched down on the polar plateau. The first American ever to set foot on the South Pole was Admiral Dufek—and he was brought there by courtesy of the same old reliable airplane that had so many other "firsts" to its credit.

The Gooney had actually become the first airplane in history to land at *both* poles, because, on May 3, 1952, an Air Force C-47 had landed at the top of the world while participating in the establishment of an ice island weather research station there.

More DC-3s were at one time in scheduled airline use than planes of any other type. In the 1950s, one hundred and seventy-four airlines in seventy nations boasted that the DC-3 was still in their fleet. Three nations—Chile, Hungary and the Netherlands—have honored the DC-3 on airmail stamps.

Flight, a British aviation magazine, said in the mid-1960s, "It is a sobering fact that numerically about thirty per cent of the world's total transport fleet consists of DC-3s." The reason was largely economic. Two feeder lines operating between large American cities in the 1960s had used DC-3s exclusively but were concerned because they were so wholly dependent upon an airplane over two decades old. New planes were ordered. After using them for several months at much higher operating costs than the old DC-3s, both lines traded them in and switched back to their old reliable money-maker—which they are still using, and still at a profit. Today, there are more than 25 U.S. air cargo and passenger airlines still flying the faithful Gooney; well over 100 foreign air carriers still use them daily.

The continued demand for DC-3s has kept their price at a high level. The first DC-3s cost American Airlines one hundred and ten thousand dollars each. Today, elegantly fitted DC-3s cannot be purchased for less than one hundred and fifty thousand dollars. To keep up with this continued usage, the Douglas Company still sells spare parts to DC-3 owners each year.

It is not surprising that the refurbished DC-3s are used by hundreds of large corporations as executive transports with exquisitely-tailored interiors. One DC-3, owned by the Houston Lumber Co., has mink-covered doorknobs, while one owned by a Texas rancher has divans and reclining chairs upholstered with unborn-calf skins. Almost all DC-3s owned by corporations or individuals are completely fitted out with galley, dressing room, beds, hi-fi, and "refreshment consoles."

N711Y, owned by Richard "Kip" DuPont of Middletown, Delaware, president of Summit Aviation, is typical of the privately owned Gooneys. Its log book shows it has over 28,000 hours on its frame; the metal placards in the cockpit show that it was originally a C-47A built in 1944 and was overhauled by Remmert-Werner into the plush luxurious paneled interior it has today. It will seat 14 passengers in super comfort: two large divans, four recliner chairs and at a dining table for four. Immaculate in appearance, it is used by DuPont to take family, friends and pets on holiday excursions to the Caribbean. The guest book signed by 711's many passengers shows trips to all of the popular resort islands plus an unusual trip to Cuba, despite Castro's anti-Yankee stand, and several visits to Central American countries.

The fancier they get, the fewer passengers the private planes hold. But the number of paying passengers being flown by the world's airlines using the DC-3 is increasing. The plane was originally designed to carry twenty-one passengers—a single row of seven single seats on one side of the aisle and a double row of fourteen seats on the other side. Today more passengers are being fitted into the same space. One airline has seated thirty-two passengers in its "new" Gooneys; another changed the size of the seats and jammed forty passengers inside. And a third has accommodated fifty passengers sitting precariously in canvas hammocks strung through the cabin.

While these passenger loads make FAA inspectors and Douglas engineers blanch, a near record number of passengers is held by a Gooney that was called upon to evacuate refugees from a Bolivian town threatened by floods in 1949. Ninety-three passengers were crammed inside. True, most of them were children, but this number of humans, plus a crew of three, made this a hard record to beat. But it was. During the Vietnam War 98 refugee orphans and five attendants were evacuated from the village of Da Lat. The three crew members aboard made this the all-time record which has yet come to our attention. This DC-3, pressed hurriedly into service to save lives, was owned by Continental Air Services and was under contract to Air Vietnam.

During World War II, 700 C-47s were "loaned" to the Soviet Union. With Douglas providing tools and plans, the Soviets produced about 3,000 more. Called at first the PS-84, it was later designated the Li-2, for its "inventor" Lissunov.

The Russian version of the Gooney Bird has been flown thousands of miles and was used by Aeroflot, the country's sole commercial airline as well as by the military tactical air arm for the paratroop force. The engines of the Li-2, also copied from the Americans, are ASH-62 radials developing 985 horsepower each. Maximum speed is estimated at 170 knots with a maximum range, at the most economical cruise speed, of 1,460 miles.

In the early 1930s, Soviet airmen startled the aviation world with their mass parachute jumps—hundreds of fully equipped soldiers leaping from scores of transport planes. So successful were their first experiments that scores of Red Army soldiers were trained in the special techniques of paratroopers. Parachuting also struck the public fancy and became a sport in Russia, with men and women learning to jump for the fun of it.

This paratroop experience stood the Soviet Army in good stead when the Nazis attacked and slowly pushed the Red forces deep within their own country. The Russians dropped highly trained guerilla fighters behind the German lines with orders to disrupt German communications, blow up trains and supply dumps, and ambush Nazi soldiers.

These famed airborne guerillas were used by the Russians all along the 1,800-mile front, wearing khaki as they leaped over the Ukraine or clad in white as they floated from planes over the snowy wastelands of the North.

Whatever their garb, the Soviet paratroopers, like the Americans in Sicily, the British in North Africa and the Australians and Americans in the South Pacific, flew in the old reliable C-47—no matter what they chose to call it.

The Russian modification of the DC-3 flew armed. Gun turrets were installed on many of them in the top of the fuselage where the navigator's astrodome is normally located. Two smaller caliber machine guns were mounted in side windows which were cut just aft of the rear door.

Very few Americans have had the privilege of flying in one of the Russian versions of the DC-3. One USAF pilot, however—Colonel Howard R. Jarrell—was accorded a rare bit of Russian hospitality when he was flown from Vladivostok to Tashkent in September 1944. Jarrell had landed a B-29 in Russian territory after a raid on Japan and was interned.

When the Russians finally decided to release Jarrell and his crew, they were brought to the airport at Vladivostok and driven to the open door of a waiting C-47. To them it was like a bit of home to see that old reliable DC-type airplane sitting there.

Curious about the Russian version and how it flew, the authors asked Jarrell about his trip.

"It wasn't a bad trip after we got used to how they flew," he said. "After take-off from Vladivostok we never got more than 100 or 200 feet above the ground for the entire three-thousand-mile trip.

"The pilots, both first lieutenants, were between thirty and forty years of age and estimated that they had about seventeen thousand flying hours each. This included all of their time in the air. Their training is progressive from ground mechanic to flight engineer, to radio operator to navigator, to copilot, and finally pilot. They do not keep separate records on how much pilot or copilot time they log.

"The weather was good all of the way as it would be almost anywhere in the world at 200 feet and every foot of it was right on top of the trans-Siberian railroad.

"There were no parachutes at all on board the plane and it's just as well. But there was one strange piece of equipment that we might do well to copy sometime. In the rear passenger cabin,

they had a potbellied stove and a cord of wood stacked neatly
beside it. The stove had handles on it so that it could be thrown
out the door in case of a bad fire.

"The turret, mounted where our navigator's astrodome is, was
manually operated and its gun was equivalent to our air-cooled
.30-caliber machine gun. The interpreter told us that it was the
only weapon necessary because no one could ever get under them
to attack. However, I understand that some models had waist
guns installed which could be manned in case of broadside attacks.

"All of the equipment, except the turret gun and stove, was
standard American equipment. All the placards were in English
as well as all of the instruments. When I asked where they had
gotten this particular C-47, our interpreter insisted that it had
been made in Russia—even when I pointed out to him that I
didn't think so because of the English signs all over it. In spite of
my logic, he insisted that it was their Li-2 and had definitely been
made in Russia.

"The way they flew that ship made my hair stand on end. All
the landing approaches were the kind our fighter pilots used to
dream of making before the days of the jets. They would zoom in
under full power at one hundred feet, rack it over in a tight bank,
yank back, and wait until the runway showed up again in front of
the nose.

"Before every flight, I noticed that the crew chief always
boarded and pre-flighted the plane before the rest of the crew
arrived. He would shut it down and disappear before the pilot
came aboard. The pilot, then, would start the engines, zoom out
to take-off position and barrel down the runway without any kind
of check. Apparently, this was standard operating procedure for
military pilots. There was never a doubt but that they liked the
airplane and had as much trust in it as did our American pilots."

In his book, *Report on the Russians*, William L. White painted
a vivid picture of the commercial version of the Soviet DC-3 from
the layman's viewpoint:

"You get aboard. There are no seat belts. There is no sign
warning against smoking; if you prefer to burn alive in a take-off

crash, that is a matter of personal conscience and no concern of the crew. Once the door slams shut, the pilot starts the motors, which have been cold since the night before. If they run at all, he releases the brakes, guns the plane on down the runway. You gather speed and clear the runway by maybe ten feet. At this instant the pilot makes his turn by the process of tilting one wing up toward the zenith and the other down until its tip is digging potatoes on the adjoining farm. Once pointed on his course he levels off and, if there are no mountains, he continues at this altitude of from 50 to 100 feet, scaring Kolkhoz cows, Sovhoz chickens, and the passengers."

The Russians were not the only ones to copy and use the Gooney during World War II. In the 1930s the Nakajima Aircraft Company of Japan had worked closely with the Douglas Aircraft Company and secured manufacturing rights for the DC-2 in 1934. Five DC-2 major airframe components were purchased; the aircraft were assembled in Japan and outfitted with Japanese flight and engine instruments. Meanwhile, one complete aircraft was bought from Great Northern Airways, a front organization for the Japanese, and shipped to Japan. All six were flown by the Japan Air Transport Company on the Fukuoka-Taipei route beginning in 1936.

In 1938 Japan obtained rights to manufacture the DC-3, ostensibly to modernize its civil air fleet. Unknown in the U.S., however, the Imperial Japanese Navy instigated the purchase because its leaders saw the aircraft's potential as a military transport. Five semi-finished fuselages and related parts were purchased from Douglas and the first DC-3, this model assembled by the Showa Airplane Company, was rolled out to the flying line in September, 1939. Simultaneously, three imported DC-3s arrived from the United States. Showa eventually built 430 DC-3s, including 75 cargo versions with reinforced flooring and wide loading door.

Several designations were given to the Japanese-built DC-2s and -3s which eventually became the L2D series. The "L2" signified transport, second Navy type, and "D" stood for Douglas. The Allies, early in the war, assigned code names to all known

Japanese aircraft to avoid identification confusion so the Japanese DC-2 became "Tess" and the DC-3 became "Tabby."

As the Japanese swung into full production with the Tabby, the shape changed slightly. Kinsei 51 engines of 1300 h.p. were added, the cowling was streamlined and the propeller was capped with a shapely spinner. Three windows were installed behind the pilot's compartment and the bulkhead behind the pilots was removed. Some models carried a blister above the forward cabin section containing a flex-mounted 13 mm machine gun and a 7 mm machine gun mounted in the rear window on each side of the fuselage. As Robert C. Mikesh, a Japanese aircraft expert at the National Air and Space Museum, noted, "These later versions had better performance than the Douglas-built model by virtue of their greater power and lighter weight."

The shortage of aircraft metals in Japan by 1943 led to substitutions that would have grayed the heads of Douglas engineers. At first, the less critical components of Tabby were redesigned and made exclusively of wood, such as the ailerons, vertical fins, rudder, horizontal stabilizer, elevators and doors. Thirty aircraft with wooden components were eventually manufactured and flown.

As the war progressed and materials became even more scarce, a single all-wooden test model, designated the L2D5, was produced. Its plywood skin was shaped as smoothly as an aluminum skin would have been but the aircraft appeared "a little boxier than the standard Gooney," according to Air Force Colonel George W. Johnson, who saw the fuselage during the Allied cleanup after hostilities. "When I first saw it," he said, "it appeared nearly ready to have engines hung on it and to be flown. I heard later that it was a static test fuselage and main wing section. The war ended before the tests could be conducted."

In the 1960s, the Federal Aviation Administration had seriously sought to encourage the aviation industry to come up with a replacement for the DC-3. Former U.S. Senator A.S. "Mike" Monroney (D-Okla.), then Chairman of the Senate Commerce Aviation Subcommittee, recommended an appropriation of $5 million to assist in the development of five prototypes in the United States. "What this country needs," he said, "is a new DC-3 that still sells at DC-3 prices." The F.A.A. established an Aircraft Department Development Service to "study the feasibility of developing a local service aircraft." At this writing at the beginning of the 1980s, the transport that can match or surpass the DC-3 in dependability and ruggedness is yet to be found.

Alan S. Boyd, then chairman of the Civil Aeronautics Board, described the requirements for the DC-3 replacement. It should:

- Carry twenty-four passengers
- Carry 1,000 pounds of cargo plus passenger baggage
- Be able to operate from runways 4,000 feet or shorter, and maybe even have vertical landing and take-off capability.
- Sell for $500,000 or less
- Operate at a cost of 60 cents or less per airplane mile.

The problem of a Gooney replacement, in spite of the technological advances since the last one was built, is involved and highly complex. Ever higher operating costs and costs of designing and engineering a new plane make the price prohibitive. In spite of Government encouragement, Government regulations have also increased the cost of a new plane, since today's airworthiness code requires many more tests and reports by the manufacturer—all of which mean more expense. Strangely, under today's F.A.A. regulations, the DC-3 could not be built in the United States now because it cannot meet all the climb requirements, is underpowered, does not meet flight control characteristics, and is too light structurally. However, a "grandfather clause" in the original 1938 airworthiness regulation has saved it. This regulation states that any type aircraft in operation before 1938 is exempt from the new requirements.

Since the early 1950s, aviation writers have used thousands of words speculating upon what the replacement for the DC-3 will be. Some have said that the large transport helicopters would do the job; others have said that advances in propulsion would enable the vertical take-off and landing planes under development to make the Gooney step aside. A few have predicted that jet engines would be made so small and yet so powerful that the replacement would either be a pure jet or a prop jet.

One anonymous writer, an old Gooney fan, summed up the difficulty in a few words:

"There's a good reason why a successful replacement for the DC-3 has never come along, and that is simply that any commercial operator who would pay new airplane prices for a new airplane with the performance and economics of a DC-3, would need to have his head read. Naturally, any carrier in his right mind who decides to replace his DC-3 is going to try to replace it with something better. There's no end to the implications of that 'something better,' and they all add up to money. When you consider that just the labor that went into building a DC-3 in the 1930s would cost many times as much today, and that the full price of a DC-3 in the thirties could hardly pay for the electronics now considered necessary, the impossibility, for economic reasons alone, of ever coming up with a 'DC-3 replacement' becomes obvious. We can't understand why people don't forget such nonsense and get behind something really worthwhile for a change. How about a return to the two-bit haircut, for instance?"

While the world's aircraft manufacturers still search diligently for a replacement, the demand for the DC-3 continues high. Modifying and updating has become big business. Most active of the original Gooney Bird renovators was the firm started in October of 1945 by Bill Remmert and Bob Werner, of St. Louis. Remmert-Werner made their first conversion of a military C-47 to a civilian DC-3 in December 1946, and subsequently converted scores of Gooneys to private business use from airline or military configuration.

As the demand for cleaned-up Gooneys continued through the years, Remmert-Werner found that their problem was not finding buyers but finding airplanes. Their search for plane skeletons and pieces widened. Since the Gooney Bird has flown in every corner of the world, there was no limit to where it might be found.

C. S. Weaks, advertising manager and chronicler for Remmert-Werner, told of the origin of some of the planes still flying as plush executive liners:

"We would put together DC-3s from parts obtained from all

over the country. We had our own fleet of large trucks, and occasionally picked up a fuselage here, right wing there, center section over yonder, and so on, until we turned up a whole airplane. I recall one plane in particular where the fuselage came from Minneapolis, the center section from Arizona, one wing from California, the other wing from Florida, the landing gear from New Jersey, the engines from our own shops, and the tail surfaces and controls from various U.S. surplus sales. It took us about three months to overhaul them all, put them together in the shape of a DC-3, dress it up, and get it in the air. It is good as new today and still flies about 800 hours per year."

Bill Remmert and Bob Werner would travel anywhere to check on the salvageability of a Gooney. Several years ago they heard about a C-47 in Japan that had been abandoned by the U.S. Air Force and given to the Japanese. The Japanese had invited bids, but Remmert-Werner passed this one up. Reason: "The successful bidder must remove aircraft from its present location 200 feet from the top of Mount Fujiyama."

The availability of this C-47 had been occasioned by the bad luck of Major John Fowle, an Air Force pilot, who had become lost in bad weather and crashed into the side of Mount Fuji in full flight. The only injury suffered in the accident was Fowle's black eye. The C-47 is still there awaiting the first enterprising soul who can figure out how to get it down. When he does, someone will be there with an offer.

While the fruitless search goes on to find a substitute for the DC-3, other modifications to the original airframe continue to give the Gooney renewed life. The Argentine Air Force, for instance, installed a jet engine in the tail which provided the aircraft with an added safety factor for takeoff and engine-out range capability, especially needed for operations in the Antarctic.

This modification includes installation of an auxillary gas turbine engine rated at 880-lb maximum thrust and a retractable air intake ahead of the vertical stabilizer that, when closed, reduces drag. When using the small jet, ground roll is reduced by 15 percent and the gross takeoff weight can be increased by 3,500 lbs. The rate of climb is also increased by about 250 feet per minute from sea level to about 6,000 feet.

While the turboprop version of the DC-3 mentioned earlier had been an aviation "first," it did not prove successful at the time (1951). But John M. Conroy, builder of strange-looking planes like the outsized Super Guppy series used to haul missiles for the U.S. space program and fuselages for the European-built A-300 jumbo jet, saw a possibility for revival of the basic idea. In 1969, he took two British-made Rolls-Royce Dart engines from a British-built Viscount and hung them on a DC-3 built in 1942. The result was the Turbo Three, a plane that one pilot described as "silky smooth and remarkably quiet in flight even though the turbo-props are noisy outside the airplane."

From the pilot's standpoint, the only noticeable difference flying the Turbo Three was that, besides a rapid acceleration during takeoff, the torque effect was to the right instead of the left. For reasons only the British engine makers know, the engines turn in the opposite direction from their American counterparts.

While the Turbo Three handles like any other DC-3 in flight, its true airspeed at 10,000 feet ranged from 182 knots at the start of a trip to 190 knots at the end. At 15,000 feet, speed increased to as much as 235 mph while jet fuel consumption reduced from 100 gallons per hour to 90.

Why would anyone want to buy a jet-age version of an "old" airplane? Jack Conroy answered the question this way:

"Both the airframe and the powerplants are the most reliable in the air today. Engine overhaul and maintenance are drastically reduced and fuel cost per mile is about the same as the piston job because of higher speed and less expensive fuel. The Turbo Three could carry higher gross weights which means greater payloads. It's faster and can fly over most weather and operate from shorter strips at higher altitudes because of power availability."

If two turboprops on a DC-3 can increase the payload, speed and altitude capabilities so much, what could three turboprops do for it?

Conroy decided to find out. On November 2, 1977, he and
veteran airline and racing pilot Clay Lacy climbed aboard a DC-3
equipped with three Pratt and Whitney PT6A-45 turboprops and
took to the California skies for another aviation "first" with the
Tri-Turbo Three. The flight not only met but exceeded even
Conroy's expectations. The Tri-Turbo Three's performance was
better than that of the two-engine version with the British-made
engines.

The Tri-Turbo Three can cruise at 230 mph and carry up to
12,000 lbs. of payload. According to Conroy, "Its increased performance, low operating costs, versatility and inexpensive ac-
quisition make the Tri-Turbo Three an ideal aircraft for performing either commercial or military missions, particularly maritime
surveillance, search and rescue, photographic or mapping missions. It also can be used for Arctic or bush operations, by
commuter airlines, or as a special purpose aircraft."

The Tri-Turbo Three has outboard wing tanks installed which
provide a range in excess of 3,000 miles. It can take off, climb to
10,000 feet cruising altitude, and with the center engine shut off,
fly a 3,000-mile mission with one hour of reserve fuel remaining.

Conroy will sell this latest version of the DC-3 for a little over
$500,000. This price includes the latest inertial navigation sys-
tem, weather radar and communications systems. Engines of
different thrust ratings can be furnished; three-, four- and five-
bladed reversible propellers are also available.

One pilot who has flown the Tri-Turbo Three commented that
"right from opening the throttles it is apparent this is not a
modified DC-3. It is a new airplane in terms of performance."

More stable at high speeds than the piston-powered Gooney,
the three-engine version is remarkably quiet inside the cabin.
The only comment that this pilot could make that might be
considered adverse is that "on three engines, it becomes noticeably heavier on the controls and response appears to be a little
slower."

In the event that a DC-3 is grounded permanently for one
reason or another, it doesn't necessarily mean that it must end up

in a smelting oven. H. L. "Smokey" Roland of Cardiff-by-the-Sea, near San Diego, California knows what to do with it. He bought a DC-3 from the Air Force airplane "boneyard" at Davis-Monthan Air Force Base, Arizona. He removed the plane's engines, nacelles, wings and tail and trucked the carcass to San Diego.

Next, he located a former Dodge school bus chassis and bolted the DC-3 fuselage firmly to the frame. He mounted a 460-cubic inch Lincoln engine between the axles and installed two 65-gallon gas tanks inside. "I had to cut off four feet of the airplane's john to get her down within the 40-foot maximum length allowed," he said. "But I can get about 10 miles to the gallon so I figure I have a cruising range of 1,300 miles without a pit stop."

Built in 1943 as No. 995 on a military contract, Roland's DC-3 mobile home was flown by Argonaut Airlines for ten years after World War II, then by Allegheny Airlines before it ended up in the plane boneyard near Tucson. According to Roland, it had been hijacked to Cuba twice during its lifetime as an airliner.

Asked how much time and money he had spent converting his Gooney Bird, Roland said, "about 3,000 hours of hard work." He estimates it's worth about $15,000 today. Describing the way people react to his creation when he cruises California freeways, he says, "They do double-takes, triple-takes and quadruple-takes."

Even the most devoted of Gooney fans know that someday the familiar purr of its engines will be silenced and its familiar shape will disappear from the skies forever. How long before that will take place is anyone's guess. The plane has already outlasted a whole generation of airline pilots and at last count was still being flown by 26 U.S. commuter and air cargo operators.

The authors, admittedly in love with the Grand Old Lady of the Skies, do not dare predict when the final flight will take place. They do say, however, that not a single person reading these words will be around on that day. In fact, the authors can confidently state that there will be a United States Air Force Gooney Bird ready to fly six centuries from now!

The proof lies buried deep beneath the snow and ice in the Swiss Alps and therein lies the final story in the incredible saga of the beloved Gooney Bird. On November 19, 1946, Major Ralph H. Tate began a flight that almost ended tragically but instead, by a strange twist of fate, will be newsworthy long afterward. On that day he filed a flight plan from Vienna, Austria, to Pisa, Italy, by way of Istres, France. On board his plane were eight passengers and a crew of four, including Tate. One of the passengers was Tate's mother, along with three wives of military personnel and an eleven-year old girl—all en route to Italy on official orders from General Mark Clark's headquarters in Vienna.

Tate, an experienced Gooney pilot, had been told that the weather on the first leg of the flight from Vienna west to Munich would be scattered clouds after the first hour of flight. Heavy snowstorms were raging in the Alps on the left of his course and, with radio aids to navigation so scarce in postwar Europe, he was not going to tempt fate by deliberately flying through them over the roughest terrain in Europe.

Take-off was uneventful and Tate went on instruments shortly afterward and began his climb to eight thousand feet where he hoped to break out on top. The Munich radio range was loud and clear as he passed overhead and continued westward. However, the reassuring sound of Munich Radio quickly faded as the plane passed behind mountain peaks and out of line-of-sight range of the ground station. He did not break out of the clouds, so he would have to continue to fly westward and then turn southward toward Istres still flying on instruments. If the Vienna weatherman's estimate of the winds aloft was correct and he could break out of the murk, there would be no problem. But if the winds were stronger than forecast and from the north instead of the west and if he didn't break out, then there were Alpine peaks waiting to take their deadly toll.

The Gooney droned on as Tate and his co-pilot, Lieutenant I. S. ("Matt") Matthews, took turns flying the instruments. Suddenly, the plane was shaken by turbulence and Tate signaled that he would take the controls. He yelled to his crew chief, Sergeant Wayne G. Folsom: "Tell the passengers to fasten their safety belts!"

The last passenger was firmly belted down when a violent updraft sent the Gooney skyrocketing. The plane shuddered a moment and then dropped like a stone. The altimeter spun backward and stopped. Out of the corner of his eye, Tate saw ominous black shapes flash by which he knew couldn't be clouds. The plane was only a few feet above the ground!

Tate jammed the throttles forward and roared back into the soup. He was again conscious of black shapes flashing by the window and then Tate felt a shock as though a bomb had gone off inside his head. In that split second he knew that they had crashed!

"Everything went white, then black, then white again," Tate told the authors. "As I passed back and forth through the gloom of semiconsciousness, I was aware of an awful silence. 'So, this is what it's like to be dead,' I said to myself. My voice scared me at first but I knew I wasn't dead then."

Tate's only injury was a gash on his head. Miraculously, the only other injury on board was a broken leg suffered by Sergeant Folsom, the crew chief. In one of the flying oddities of all time, Tate's airplane had crashed in the Alps in full flight with no loss of life. To add to the miracle, the Gooney was not seriously damaged and could be easily repaired.

While the luck of this dozen people had held out in the inadvertent "landing," they still faced incredible odds in surviving the subzero cold so far off the beaten track of civilization and with no hope of rescue until the weather cleared. There was no cold-weather survival equipment on board and no food save a few candy bars. Fortunately, a fire could be kindled and kept going by burning everything that would ignite.

It was several days before the weather cleared and search planes located the luckless Gooney and dropped supplies. When the plane was pinpointed among the peaks and crags, it was found to be resting on the only high plateau within many miles. Within a hundred yards in every direction were hidden crevices covered by snow bridges.

Even though spotted from the air, Tate and his charges could not yet be rescued. Swiss mountaineers had to spend several days fighting their way to the treacherous plateau before they finally were able to evacuate the anxious Americans. After the rescue the weather closed in for the next twelve days and heavy snowstorms covered the whole Alpine region. Within a hundred miles of the scene not a single plane got off the ground. When pilots flew over the crash site two weeks later, not a trace of the plane could be found.

The crash, search and rescue of Major Ralph Tate and his crew and passengers made world headlines and added a footnote to history as well. Never before had a transport plane crashed in the Alps without killing everyone aboard. The rescue was also a history-making effort which once again proved the courage, determination and stamina of the Swiss mountaineers.

The world soon forgot the incident but not the Swiss. They collected the pictures, magazines and newspapers featuring the crash and rescue and placed them in their famous museum at Bern. The next spring, those who had participated in the operation climbed back up to the plateau and located the plane by probing through the snow with long poles. Digging down, they opened the escape hatch in the top of the cockpit and placed a sealed capsule inside on the throttle quadrant. In this capsule were copies of the magazines and newspapers, telling the whole sequence of events. The hatch was then closed and the blowing snow soon covered the site again.

To the Swiss this gesture had a purpose. This rescue had been a classic from beginning to end, with literally hundreds of people of several nationalities pitching in to save lives. But there was another reason for the trek back to the plateau. The plateau was part of a glacier, and Swiss glaciologists believe that Tate's airplane will sink slowly through the glacial ice until it reaches a point where it will slide downhill and eventually spit itself out at the bottom—completely intact. The estimate is that the plane will take six hundred years to do this. So, knowing the tendency of the Gooney Bird to stay around and make history, it is safe to say that shortly after the turn of the 26th century, the plane will again make newspaper headlines around the world. There is no reason to believe that whoever finds it then will think it too quaint to fly. Who knows? They may still be looking for an airplane to replace the DC-3 and may well conclude, as we do now in the 20th century, that the only replacement for a DC-3 is another DC-3.

Appendix 1. Evolution of the DC-3

Civil Versions

DC-1   Carried 12 passengers. Wright engines. 1 built.

DC-2   Carried 14 passengers. One delivered with Pratt & Whitney Hornet engines; two with Bristol Pegasus VI engines; the rest had Wright engines. 130 built.

DST   Skysleeper model with 14 berths. Wright engines.

DST-A   Skysleeper model with 14 berths. Pratt & Whitney engines.

DC-3   Delivered to airlines and non-military customers. Wright engines. 455 built pre-war.

DC-3A   DC-3 with Pratt & Whitney engines.

DC-3B   Half Skysleeper, half seats. Pratt & Whitney engines.

DC-3C   This designation initially referred to C-47 military versions purchased from the U.S. Government that were completely remanufactured with new serial numbers. Later, surplus C-47s that were updated to the DC-3C configuration also carried this designation.

DC-3D   Originally were C-117s built as passenger aircraft rather than as cargo planes. At the conclusion of WWII, Douglas purchased parts from undelivered C-117 stock from U.S. Government and remanufactured them as DC-3Ds with new serial numbers.

DC-3S   Designation given to DC-3 aircraft converted to Super DC-3s.

Military Versions

XC-32   DC-2; carried 14 passengers. Wright engines. 1 built.

C-32A   DC-2 aircraft impressed from the airlines during WWII. Wright engines. 24 had this designation.

C-33	Same as DC-2 with larger tail and cargo door. Wright engines. 18 built.
C-34	Same as DC-2 with VIP interior furnishings. 2 built.
C-38	C-33 with DC-3 tail. 1 converted.
C-39	DC-2 (C-33) aircraft with DC-3 landing gear and tail. Wright engines. 35 built.
C-41 and C-41A	DC-3s with VIP interiors. 1 of each built.
C-42	Same as C-39 with VIP interior. Wright engines. 1 built.
C-47	DC-3 with cargo door and floor. Pratt & Whitney engines. 953 built.
C-47A	C-47 with 24-volt electrical system. Pratt & Whitney engines. 4,931 built.
C-47B	C-47 with two-stage blower for high altitude operation. Pratt & Whitney engines. 3,241 built.
C-47C	Amphibian model equipped with Edo floats. Pratt & Whitney engines. At least two and possibly more converted from C-47Cs.
C-47D	C-47B without blowers. Pratt & Whitney engines. Converted from available C-47Bs.
C-47E	Equipped with electron equipment for checking radio aids to navigation. Pratt & Whitney engines. 6 converted.
YC-47F	Redesignated from YC-129 and transferred to U.S. Navy as R4D-8. Wright engines. 1 converted.
C-48	DC-3A originally built for United Air Lines. Pratt & Whitney engines. 1 built.
C-48A	DC-3A with plush interior. Pratt & Whitney engines. 3 built.
C-48B	Same as DST-A Skysleeper. Pratt & Whitney engines. 16 built.
C-48C	Same as DC-3A. Pratt & Whitney engines. 16 built.
C-49	DC-3 built for TWA with 24 passenger seats. Wright engines. 6 built.
C-49A	DC-3 built for Delta Air Lines with 21 seats. Wright engines. 3 built.

C-49B	Navy R4D-2 built originally for Eastern Airlines; door on right side. Wright engines. 3 built.
C-49C	Troop carrier version with small door, side seats. Originally built for Delta Air Lines. Wright engines. 2 built.
C-49D	Same as C-49C; built for Eastern Air Lines. Wright engines. 11 built.
C-49E thru H	DC-3s originally ordered by the airlines and converted to troop carriers. Wright engines. 58 built.
C-49J and K	DC-3s with side seating for troops. Wright engines. 57 built.
C-50	DC-3 built for American Airlines. 21 passengers. Wright engines. 4 built.
C-50A	DC-3s built for American Airlines converted to troop carrier interior. Wright engines. 2 built.
C-50B	DC-3s built for Braniff International. Same as C-50A with minor interior changes. Wright engines. 3 built.
C-50C	DC-3 built for Penn-Central Airlines; passenger interior. Wright engines. 1 built.
C-50D	DC-3s built for Penn-Central Airlines, converted to troop carrier interior. Wright engines. 4 built.
C-51	DC-3 built for Canadian-Colonial Airlines; troop carrier interior. Whitney engines. 1 built.
C-52	DC-3A built for United Air Lines; troop carrier interior with right hand door. Pratt & Whitney engines. 1 built.
C-52A	DC-3A built for Western Airlines; troop carrier interior. Pratt & Whitney engines. 2 built.
C-52B	DC-3A built for United Air Lines; troop carrier interior. Pratt & Whitney engines. 2 built.
C-52C	DC-3A built for Eastern Airlines; troop carrier interior. Pratt & Whitney engines. 1 built.
C-53	Troop transport given name of Skytrooper. Pratt & Whitney engines. 193 built.
XC-53A	Experimental model with hot air wing and tail de-icing system; full span flaps. Pratt & Whitney engines. 1 converted.

C-53B	Special winterized version for arctic operations. Pratt & Whitney engines. 8 built.
C-53C	C-53 with minor interior changes. Pratt & Whitney engines. 17 built.
C-53D	C-53 with 24-volt system. Pratt & Whitney engines. 159 built.
C-68	DC-3A with 21-passenger interior. Wright engines. 2 built.
C-84	Originally built as DC-3B (half Skysleeper, half passenger seat configuration). 4 aircraft impressed from airlines.
C-117A and B	Passenger version similar to C-47B. Pratt & Whitney engines. 17 built as C-117As then 8 reworked to include two-stage blower and designated as C-117B.
C-117C	C-47 type aircraft loaned to airlines which put in passenger interiors. When returned to Army Air Forces, they were re-designated C-117Cs.
C-117D	*See* YC-129.
YC-129	Redesignated YC-47F and then Navy R4D-8. Wright engines. 1 converted. Now designated as C-117D.
XCG-17	C-47 with engines removed and used as a glider. 1 converted.

NOTE: All C-49 through C-52, plus the C-68 and C-84 aircraft were airline transports impressed from the airlines or at the factory prior to delivery.

Approximately 600 DC-3 type aircraft were procured for the U.S. Navy by the Army Air Forces Materiel Command during World War II. Given the general designation of R4D, they were used for transportation of personnel and cargo. The several models numbered R4D-1 through R4D-8 were equivalent to the AAF variants from the C-47 through the C-53 models.

Prior to World War II the U.S. Navy purchased five DC-2s which were designated R2D-1s.

After the war, Douglas converted 105 C-47 or DC-3 type aircraft to Super DC-3s. Two were Douglas prototype and sales aircraft. The first was reworked from the YC-129 to YC-47F and finally the R4D-8 (now designated as the C-117D). Three DC-3S aircraft were sold to Capital Airlines and 100 (in addition to the R4D-8) were converted for the U.S. Navy.

Appendix 2.
U.S. air carriers
using DC-3s*

AAT Airlines
1129 Simonton Street
Key West, Florida 33040

Aero Dyne Corp.
300-400 Airport Way
Renton, Washington 98055

Aero Virgin Islands Corp.
Box 546
St. Thomas, Virgin Islands 00801

Aeroluz International Airways
Suite 500
403 Madison Street
Tampa, Florida 33602

Air Atlantic, Inc.
Box 336
Danvers, Maine 01923

Air Caribbean
International Airport
Isla Verda, Puerto Rico 00913

Air Institute & Service
Southern Illinois Airport
Carbondale, Illinois 62901

Air Polynesia
Box 30526
Honolulu, Hawaii 96820

Airgo, Inc.
Box 31
Love Field Terminal Building
Dallas, Texas 75235

Airlift, Inc.
3711 Truman Street
El Paso, Texas 79930

Argosy Air Lines, Inc.
4161 SW 11th Terrace
Ft. Lauderdale, Florida 33315

Baron Aviation Service
Rolla National Airport
Box 518
Vichy, Missouri 65580

Ed Boardman Flying Service
Meacham Field
Ft. Worth, Texas 76106

BO-S-Aire Airlines
Rt. 9, Box 287D
Anderson, South Carolina 29621

Bonanza Airlines Corp.
Box H-3
Sardy Field
Aspen, Colorado 81611

Catalina Air Freight
13950 Triple B Road #1
Greenwell Springs, Louisiana 70739

Central American Air Taxi, Inc.
Bowman Field
Louisville, Kentucky 40205

Charter Air Center
Regional Airport
Box 1334
Gainesville, Florida 32602

Corporate Jet Aviation
1951 Airport Road
Atlanta, Georgia 30341

Cryderman Air Service
7002 Highland Road
Pontiac, Michigan 48054

Don Air Services
Municipal Airport
Alliance, Nebraska 69301

Evergreen Air of Montana, Inc.
Box 4345
Missoula, Montana 59806

Florida Airlines, Inc.
Box 13084
Airgate Station
Sarasota, Florida 33578

Gay Airways Inc.
International Airport
Box 6003
Anchorage, Alaska 99502

International Airways, Inc.
Smyrna Airport
Box 17096
Nashville, Tennessee 37217

JAARS, Inc.
Box 248
Waxhaw, North Carolina 28173

Meridian Air Cargo
Municipal Airport
Box 30079
Memphis, Tennessee 38130

Morgan Air Transport
Box 71
Pensacola, Florida 32591

Naples Airlines
Municipal Airport
Box 1037
Naples, Florida 33940

National Jet Services, Inc.
Indianapolis International Airport
Box 41714
Indianapolis, Indiana 46241

Nevada Airlines
Box 19419
Las Vegas, Nevada 89119

Pacific American Airlines
Box 408
Monrovia, California 91016

*Current list as of spring, 1979.

Pinehurst Airlines
Pinehurst-Southern Pines Airport
Box 911
Pinehurst, North Carolina 28374

Provincetown-Boston Airlines
Municipal Airport
Box 639
Provincetown, Massachusetts 02657

Sedalia-Marshall-Boonville Stage Line
5805 Fleur Drive
Des Moines, Iowa 50321

Shawnee Airlines
Box 52-2910
Miami, Florida 33152

Skyway Aviation
Box 67
Ft. Leonard Wood, Missouri 65473

Spokane Airways
International Airport
Box 19125
Building 700
Spokane, Washington 99219

Stevens Beechcraft, Inc.
Box 589
Grear, South Carolina 29651

Summit Airlines
Philadelphia International Airport
Philadelphia, Pennsylvania 19153

Trans-Florida Airlines
Bin 10150, West Side Station
Daytona Beach, Florida 32020

Tropics International, Inc.
Box 520616
Miami, Florida 33152

Vero Monmouth Airlines
Box 1985
Vero Beach, Florida 32960

Viking International Airlines
7000—34th Avenue South
Minneapolis, Minnesota 55450

Index